For Mummy
So brave and so beautiful
Wendy Ann Gale (née Silver)
13 June 1931 to 6 December 1998

THIS IS A CARLTON BOOK

Design copyright © 2000 Carlton Books Limited
Text copyright © 2000 Fiona & Keith Baker

This edition was published by Carlton Books Limited in 2000
20 Mortimer Street
London W1N 7RD

A CIP catalogue for this book is available from the British Library

ISBN 1 85868 875 2

Editorial Manager: Venetia Penfold
Art Director: Penny Stock
Editors: Alice Whately and Zia Mattocks
Editorial Assistant: Kate Paver
Design: Mercer Design
Picture Manager: Lorna Ainger
Production Manager: Garry Lewis

Printed and bound in Dubai

C20th

furniture

Fiona & Keith Baker

CARLTON
BOOKS

Contents

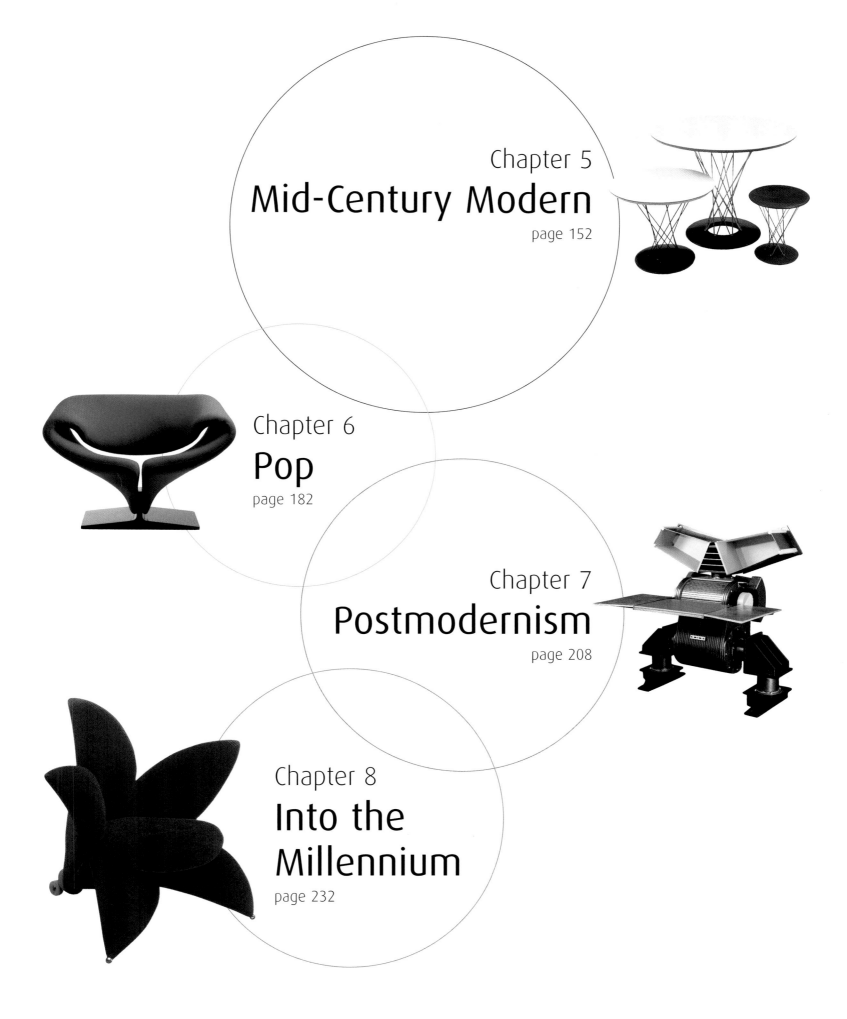

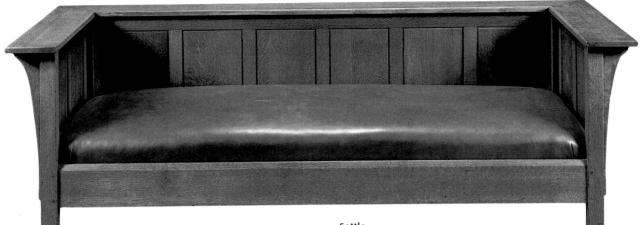

Settle
c 1912 Leopold Stickley and John George Stickley

Carved Mahogany Vitrine
c 1900 Hector Guimard

Sheet-Steel Chair
c 1928 René Prou

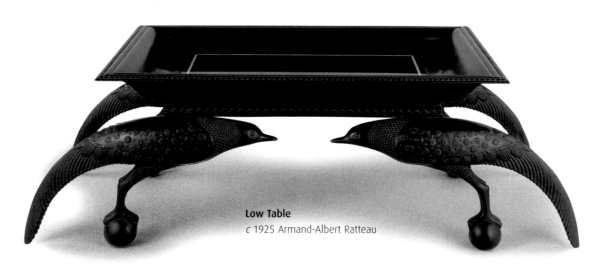

Low Table
c 1925 Armand-Albert Ratteau

Introduction

Furniture is an important part of the human environment, it brings order and form to our daily lives – from the bed we sleep in to the table we eat at. The interior of our homes is the only environment over which we have any real control. We are born into a world at a specific time in history, to a country with its own landscape, to our parents' house in a given location, to school and work. The environments that go with these are largely beyond our choosing unless we are a politician or an architect, perhaps.

When we buy our first home we are finally masters of our own space – it is ours to do with what we will. We are free to express our tastes and interests in the colours, furniture, pictures, textiles and objects we choose, limited only by our budget. Our homes are of vital importance; when we walk through the front door we enter a domain we have tried to make comfortable and peaceful. Furniture plays a dominant role in this because it occupies a large part of our living environment. It is also very expensive.

In the course of history many pieces of furniture become dust, but some are treasured and revered by future generations. This book contains many pieces that have achieved that venerated status. These pieces also reflect our social history, as styles of a particular age evolve from the society that engendered them – sometimes as the development from a preceding era and sometimes as a reaction against it. Modernism, for example, is the antithesis of Art Nouveau.

We begin this book with the Arts and Crafts Movement – a school of design that had a profound impact on twentieth-century furniture and furnishings. One of its major legacies was to make people more design-conscious, and through the teaching and work of its leading exponents the status of the applied arts was once more elevated closer to fine art. This occurred because most of the Movement's leading lights were architects or artists, all of whom had design skills. In the second half of the nineteenth century the likes of William Morris realized that many of the people responsible for the manufacture of the chattels available for popular consumption did not possess these skills. Even if they were unable to prevent machine and mass production (which the Arts and Crafts Movement was vehemently against), they did acknowledge the need for professionally trained designers in the applied arts. The twentieth century was the era of the designer, and culminated in the veneration and status of the designer label.

The continental Art Nouveau Movement was born partly out of the Arts and Crafts Movement and partly out of a desire to move away from historicism. At its best, it is surely one of the most appealing and beautiful of styles, especially when you look at the work of Hector Guimard and Louis Majorelle. The design ethos did not last a particularly long time, but it did leave a distinctive legacy, illustrating the fact that decoration and form can be beautifully united in the hands of a great designer.

Initially, the transition from the nineteenth to the twentieth century was a slow one. Things speeded up following the First World War, and the 1920s saw the beginning of the Modern era. Art Deco was born, and its distinctive form and exotic quality reflected the style, affluence and glamour of the 1920s and 1930s perfectly. Developing alongside it was Modernism – a principled school of uncluttered design that endeavoured to offer good and functional furniture to all. It is almost as if Art Deco and Modernism took the two main principles of the Arts and Crafts Movement and split them in half: Art Deco took the quality, love of materials and craftsmanship, and Modernism embraced the concept of 'fitness for purpose'.

The Second World War closed the chapter on Art Deco but post-war design retained the rational and functional ethos of Modernism, endowing it with a more organic and humane approach. In addition, bright colours were introduced as a backlash to the darkness of the war years. Design was lighter and reflected the new egalitarianism and optimism about the future.

The 1960s created innovative and fun furniture that reflected a rapidly changing and fashion-conscious society. This exuberance was slightly diluted during the ecologically minded 1970s, but there remained a greater sense of freedom and the eccentricities of both the designer and the consumer seemed to have no limit.

Postmodernism in the 1980s reintroduced decoration and colour in a big way. The decade of economic success nourished a society unafraid of spending or displaying its wealth. The recession of the late 1980s resulted in a more cautious approach during the 1990s, while both decades produced furniture that had an increased reliance on sculptural form.

If the designer has risen to prominence during the twentieth century then mention should also be made of the far-sighted manufacturers and retail outlets who helped to promote them. L'Art Nouveau Bing, Liberty, and Heal & Sons were all leaders in their fields, with in-house workshops and commissioned designers (in the case of Heal & Sons, Sir Ambrose Heal himself). Knoll Associates and Herman Miller deserve a special mention because the list of designers they commissioned reads like a who's who of post-war talent.

During the 1920s and 1930s large department stores, particularly in France (Au Printemps, Galerie Lafayete, Louvre and Au Bon Marche) and America (R H Macy & Co. and Lord & Taylor), actively supported and promoted the Art Deco Movement. In more recent times we have had 'design concept' stores such as Habitat, The Conran Shop and IKEA – the Swedish superstore responsible for taking Scandinavian design across the world.

Besides world events and artistic movements, another important impact on design has been the development of new materials such as tubular steel, chromium-plating, stainless steel, nylon, polyurethane and foam rubber. These have all offered designers the chance to create lighter, more resilient structures, as well as allowing greater freedom of form, usually at more economically viable prices. Mass-production methods have also had a major effect on furniture, and the manufacturing of a piece has become an integral part of the design process.

If new manufacturing techniques have increased the design brief, then so too have ecological considerations, with the preservation of natural resources and recycling of man-made materials primary considerations. Consumer rights and safety have also become important issues when considering the final product.

Historically, expensive one-offs produced by individual craftsman were opposed by the Modernists who favoured mass production. Today, however, there is a move towards limited production runs, offering people the opportunity to acquire more exclusive pieces at affordable prices.

The twentieth century has produced many beautiful, creative and innovative pieces of furniture and the exciting effect of new materials and technology is surely a benchmark for new developments in the next century. Our young son thinks interactive furniture is the way forward. Whether he is right remains to be seen, but if the twenty-first century produces as much variety and invention as the twentieth century did, design students are definitely in for a treat.

'Listen To Me' Couch
1947 Edward J Wormley

Ribbon Chair
1965 Pierre Paulin

Atlantis Armchair
1989 Mark Brazier-Jones

Felt Chair
1994 Marc Newson

Chapter 1

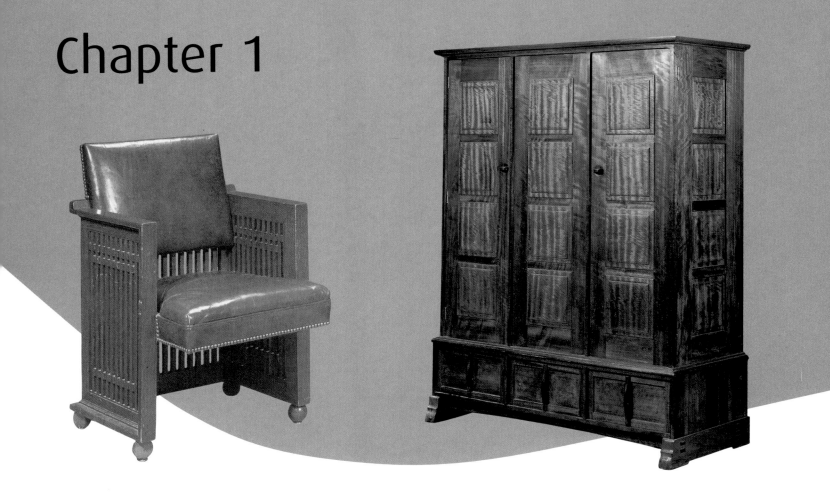

Arts and Crafts

The Arts and Crafts Movement, with its adherence to the principle of 'fitness for purpose', was born in the nineteenth century from a complex seedbed that grew to express itself in the latter part of the century and the Edwardian era of the next. Indeed, the influence is still felt today, with some designers continuing to follow along the Arts and Crafts path.

The Industrial Revolution had dramatically changed Western culture. The growth of the middle classes led to a massive increase in the housing market and Victorian Britain was manufacturing huge quantities of wallpaper, furniture and furnishings to satisfy the demand. This, however, led to the separation of the 'maker' from the 'buyer', which saw a reduction in design quality and construction. Factory production did little for the quality of life of its workers, either. Although some cabinet-makers remained, much of the output was machine-produced copies of earlier designs.

The Arts and Crafts Movement began in Britain. A W N Pugin, John Ruskin and Charles Robert Ashbee all played a part in promoting the new aesthetic, but William Morris was the pivotal figure. 'Have nothing in your house except what you know to be useful or believe to be beautiful,' he said.

'Fitness for purpose' sums up one of the major principles of the Arts and Crafts Movement. It means that the design of a piece of

furniture should suit its function and be practical. The materials and method should be the most appropriate, and reflect the maker's craft. Prior to machinery, part of the craftsman's job was to conceal the evidence of his hand, but as machines duplicated ancient skills this was reversed in order to show the piece was handmade. Decoration was permissible, but not to excess.

There were many influences within the Movement, including the medieval, which promoted the skilled craftsman, whose integrity towards design and materials was much admired, and which supported the 'socialist' argument against the horrors of machine-induced drudgery. The proportions and quality of English vernacular furniture and the Aesthetic Movement, which was often inspired by the simplicity of Japanese design, also played

their part. Linked with the medieval influence was the Gothic Revival, viewed by Pugin as both 'strong and hospitable'.

In America, the ratio of influences was slightly different but the real discrepancy was a more tolerant approach to machinery. If used judiciously it could take the grind out of laborious tasks, leaving the craftsman more time to use his skill. It also had a major impact on economic viability.

The term Arts and Crafts came from The Arts and Crafts Exhibition Society. It is thought that the seeds for the Society were sown by John Ruskin, who wrote to William Morris in 1878: 'How much good might be done by the establishment of an exhibition anywhere, in which the Right doing, instead of the Clever doing, of all that men know to do, should be the test of acceptance.'

Mahogany Occasional Table

Date: *c* 1890

Designer: **George Jack (1855–1932)**

Made by: **Morris & Co. (1874–1940)**

The mahogany table, with its serpentine circular top and arched apron beneath, stands on gently curved supports that taper towards oval pad feet. The dominant design element of the table is the curved line – even the stretchers are curved and united by a circle carved as a flower head. The effect is subtly organic and 'natural', and this is highlighted by the carved leaf detail on the upper part of the table's legs.

The table was designed by George Jack for Morris & Co. and is typical of the furniture firm's later pieces – the early ones being more robust and medieval-looking.

William Morris helped to focus the architect's eye on the interior and furnishings of a house, and brought greater recognition to the 'applied arts'. This piece comes from the drawing room of Standen in Sussex. The house was designed by architect Philip Webb, who was Morris & Co.'s chief designer for many years; he was succeeded by George Jack. Usually the table stands on a Morris & Co. hand-woven carpet, and the vase (pictured) on top of the table is by William de Morgan, a leading ceramist, whose tiles are featured in many of Morris's interiors.

Table with Ebony and Holly Inlay

Date: **1892**

Designer: **William R Lethaby (1857–1931)**

Commissioned by: **Lord Manners for Avon Tyrell**

House, Hampshire

The legs on this table are quite distinctive and different from other Arts and Crafts pieces. The squared-knopping is repeated in larger form on the feet which, unusually, are made of brass, making them less susceptible to dents and scuffs than wood. The golden colour of the brass is picked up by the pale colour of the holly inlay.

To prevent the table top from being totally plain, the English designer used a framed construction, and inlaid the edge with ebony dots. This gives the table a stronger definition which, together with the decorated apron, balances the top and bottom. The apron is inlaid with a repeating,

feathered-arrow pattern in holly and ebony. Initially, it looks as if the apron is tapered on the end sections, but this is not the case. The two central pairs of legs are, in fact, set wider than the end ones; you can see this if you look at the stretchers.

Walnut and Cane-Seated Chair

Date: **c 1895**

Designer: **Sir Lawrence Alma-Tadema OM, RA**

(1836–1912)

It is not certain when Sir Lawrence Alma-Tadema designed this chair, but following his death 15 of them were sold at an auction of the contents of his house in St John's Wood, London. A Royal Academician, he was known to have designed and adapted some furniture for his own use. He used the shape of his easel as a decorative device and this motif was even to be found on nail heads.

The walnut chair has a lightness to the frame, accentuated by the openness of the back and the holes in the cane seat. The eye is immediately drawn to the back, but the tapering legs and the stretchers maintain the balance. The splat, which is structurally important as well as supporting the sitter's back, is boldly egocentric, featuring a fluid and beautifully executed combination of Alma-Tadema's monogram and the easel motif.

Writing Cabinet

Date: **1898**

Designer: **Charles Robert Ashbee**

(1863–1942)

Made by: **Guild of Handicraft**

Workshop, London

One of Charles Robert Ashbee's most elaborate pieces, this mahogany cabinet appears much bigger than its measurements: 1.46 m (4 ft 9½ in) tall by 1.07 m (3½ ft) wide. The plain-framed and panelled construction contrasts with the delicate metalwork, highlighted by leather backing. Perhaps this is part of the attraction. The metalwork hints at further surprises on opening the doors, where the pale holly interior strikes a contrast to the dark exterior, and is inlaid with carved mahogany blooms – just the thing to inspire the writer.

Ashbee, an English architect and designer, was a leading figure in the Arts and Crafts Movement. He founded the Guild and School of Handicraft in London in 1887, which he then moved to Gloucestershire in 1902. The aim was to establish a medieval-style community of craftsmen, but it proved economically difficult to sustain and was disbanded in 1908.

The Kelmscott Chaucer Cabinet

Date: **1899**

Designer: **Charles Francis Annesley Voysey**

(1857–1941)

Made by: **F C Coote**

English architect and designer Charles Francis Annesley Voysey was a master of understatement and a leading light in the Arts and Crafts Movement. Voysey's houses were characterized by an openness and lightness which is immensely attractive, and his furniture is approachable and comfortable.

Without the brass hinges and panels the cabinet is seemingly plain. However, with simple details Voysey elevates the cabinet beyond the ordinary. If the cornice was reduced rather than extended, or the apron on the base was straight rather than curved and the legs not tapered, the balance and the nature of the cabinet would be completely altered. It would be heavy and ponderous.

The cabinet was made to store William Morris's Kelmscott printing of Chaucer's works. The interior is painted in red and there is red suede beneath the exterior brass lettering. The brass work was probably executed by Thomas Elsley & Co., and is perfectly weighted. The heart-shaped terminals to the strap hinges and the bird motif within are both typical Voysey decorations.

The 'Lovat' Toilet Table

Date: **1899**

Designer: **George Henry Walton**

(1867–1933)

The walnut toilet table, with mirrors and linen hangings, was part of a range of furniture that grew out of various private commissions. (A similar toilet table and washstand was exhibited by the Scottish architect and designer at the Glasgow International Exhibition of 1901.)

This piece is typical of George Henry Walton's work at the turn of the century, illustrating his distinctive use of the cabriole leg at the front and heart-shaped cutouts above the mirrors. The motif stencilled on the linen hangings was also used in different variations by Walton.

At the age of 21, Walton opened an interior decorating firm in Glasgow. Hoping to build on this success, he went to London and was asked to decorate the showrooms of the Dudley Gallery for a photographic exhibition in 1897, and this was swiftly followed by the Eastman (Kodak) Photographic Exhibition at the New Galleries. Walton went on to design both Kodak's showrooms and their packaging.

Oak Dresser

Date: *c* 1900

Designed and made by: **Liberty & Co.**

This dresser is typical of Liberty's Arts and Crafts pieces. Made from planks of quarter-sawn oak, it has an extended cornice with a shaped apron and shelves below. The top of the base is also extended, to give a pronounced overhang. The tops of the fielded panelled doors are curved to repeat the line of the apron.

Liberty was founded in 1875 by Arthur Lasenby Liberty. The firm started out as an Oriental emporium, but soon began to commission Arts and Crafts fabrics. The furniture department was established in 1884, followed by silver, pewter and jewellery ranges, which were all designed in-house.

Individual designers were not promoted at the time, but Liberty was successful because they commissioned or employed talented designers. Sir Arthur, as he became, also had the ability to recognize trends and was not adverse to taking advantage of the machine, unlike C R Ashbee and the Guild of Handicraft.

Oak Bureau

Date: *c* 1900

Designer: **Charles Rohlfs (1853–1936)**

Made by: **Charles Rohlfs Workshop, USA**

American designer Charles Rohlfs's inimitable style is perfectly demonstrated here. A thwarted actor, his work is like a narrative holding different characters together.

In the case of this bureau, the unique blend of elements – including Arts and Crafts, Art Nouveau, medieval and Norwegian – is pure Rohlfs. The piece is constructed from planks of quarter-sawn oak and has a fall-front enclosing shelves and drawers. Like a Davenport, there are drawers on one side, and a cupboard on the other to which Rohlfs has added a bookshelf at the back. In addition, the desk revolves on its base, so that every feature is accessible without the user having to rise from his chair.

Nails are decorative as well as functional, and the main panel is pierced with a stylized repeating pattern. Continuing the decorative theme, the fall-front and side panels are carved with a sinuous curvilinear decoration, and the finials are flowingly Art Nouveau.

Rohlfs's work was well received in Europe. He produced a set of chairs for Buckingham Palace and was made a fellow of the Royal Society of Arts.

Walnut Rush-Seated Chair

Date: *c* 1900

Designer: **Walter Cave (1863–1939)**

This chair is wonderfully organic in a restrained Arts and Crafts way. More contained than its continental Art Nouveau equivalent, the curved uprights extend down to splayed feet and up to splayed finials. These are united by curved horizontal splats, the lower of which is united to the drop-in rush seat by vertical slats. The seat is angled and enclosed by a broad apron, and the curved front legs taper towards the feet which are united by stretchers.

An architect and designer, Walter Cave's early work was influenced by fellow English architect Charles Francis Annesley Voysey – particularly after he took over one of Voysey's commissions in 1897. This chair shows a little of Voysey's influence, but the curved verticals make the piece Cave's own. The bud-like variation on the finials is a device he also used on other chairs and settles.

Walnut Veneered Three-Fold Screen

Date: *c* 1901

Designer: **George Logan (1866–1939)**

Made by: **Wylie & Lockhead, Glasgow**

This folding screen won Scottish designer George Logan a silver medal at the Turin International Exhibition in 1902. It was made by Wylie & Lockhead – the firm Logan joined in 1882 – and includes a watercolour-and-ink drawing by Jessie M King at the top of the centrefold.

The luxurious decoration on the walnut panels complements the drawing, with delicate applications of silver, mother-of-pearl, stones described as red amethyst and turquoise. The side-folds are pierced at the top with oval apertures framed with silver, and the top of each fold has an extended point. This pointed motif is repeated at the bottom in carved and pierced forms.

Logan continued to work for Wylie & Lockhead until 1937. The firm was the most important commercial manufacturer of 'Glasgow style' furniture, and also employed the designers E A Taylor and John Ednie.

Display Cabinet

Date: *c* 1902

Designer: **George Jack (1855–1932)**

Made by: **Morris & Co.**

George Jack was born in America but came to Britain in the early 1870s. He joined Philip Webb's practice in 1880 and became chief furniture designer at Morris & Co. a decade later. His pieces were more traditional, with a distinct eighteenth-century feel to them. He frequently used inlay as a form of decoration.

This cabinet in Honduras mahogany is made to a very high standard. It has foliate decoration of inlaid holly on the pediment and holly and ebony stringing framing the drawers and panels. The glazing bars are also used as a decorative device, rather than leaving the doors plain. Overall, the piece is statuesque, refined and eminently suitable for a drawing room. According to the Morris & Co. catalogue, the cabinet could have been bought in 1911 for £102 18s 0d.

Oak Hall Chair

Date: *c* 1902

Designer: **Bernard Ralph Maybeck (1862–1957)**

American architect Bernard Ralph Maybeck aimed to create buildings that blended with their locality in terms of design and materials. He is best known for his timber-framed chalets in Berkeley, California, where he concentrated his energies on buildings and structure, rather than interior design and furnishings.

This hall chair is attributed to Maybeck because of its similarity to a set of a dining chairs he designed for Phoebe Hearst in 1902. Hearst's house was built like a hill-top castle, and her dining room included a long refectory table and tall chairs with medieval-style 'keyhole' backs.

The chairs were carved from solid oak planks, cut and shaped for effect and united to show their simple exposed construction. This chair would not have looked out of place in Philip Webb's Red House, built in 1860 for William Morris, which was also furnished with medieval-inspired pieces.

Oak Display Cabinet

Date: **1902**

Designer: **Edward George Punnett (1862–1948)**

Made by: **William Birch, High Wycombe, England**

This cabinet is constructed from plain oak planks. The pediment is simply cut for visual effect and there is no elaborate adornment. The central plank begins and ends with an inlaid floral motif and the symmetry of the cabinet is established by two similar motifs on either side. The shelves at the top are partly enclosed and the arched tops are repeated on the front and side apron of the base. The supports, with their cut-out segments, are united by an under-shelf, and opaque green and white glass is geometrically leaded in the doors.

The Cabinet Maker noted in its June 1886 edition that William Birch was one of the best-managed factories in the furniture-producing town of High Wycombe. It was a leading producer of commercial Arts and Crafts furniture. English designer Edward George Punnett initially worked as a designer for J S Henry before joining William Birch and was known to have produced work on commission for Liberty & Co. that was also made by Birch.

Ebonized Cabinet

Date: **1902**

Designer: **Mackay Hugh Baillie Scott**

(1865–1945)

Made by: **Dresdener Werkstätten für**

Handwerkskunst, Germany

The simplicity of the decorative scheme on this cabinet cannot be faulted. The unassuming ebonized form is effectively brought to life by the stylized foliate design and the silvered-metal hinges and lock plates, which are embossed with flower heads.

Inside, the cabinet has banks of smaller drawers with similar silver handles. The smaller, centralized cupboard has a simpler variation of the exterior inlay on the front, and an interior of pear wood. The doors are painted and lacquered in purple, cream and yellowy green, with a formalized leaf and flower design. The inside face of each of the main doors is inlaid with ivory squares, each composed of four triangles, centred with a square of abalone.

The cabinet was made to a high standard and was part of a very productive collaboration between Baillie Scott and the Dresdener Werkstätten. The Scottish designer had won a commission to redecorate several rooms for the Grand Duke of Hesse's Palace at Darmstadt in 1896, marking the beginning of his involvement with the German Arts and Crafts Movement.

Oak Bureau

Date: *c* 1903

Designer: **E A Taylor (1874–1951)**

Made by: **Wylie & Lockhead, Glasgow**

High-sided furniture was particularly popular at the turn of the century and this oak bureau reflects the fashion. Created by E A Taylor, it illustrates two of the Scotsman's design specialities – furniture and stained glass.

Demonstrating the simplicity of Arts and Crafts design, the bureau has plain sides that extend down to form the legs. The rest is fairly conventional, except for the high sides and panels of stained glass, which show the influence of the Glasgow Four: Charles Rennie Mackintosh, Margaret MacDonald, Frances MacDonald and Herbert McNair. The bureau appears in the Wylie & Lockhead catalogue of 1903, where it could be bought in light or ebonized oak or mahogany.

Taylor worked for Wylie & Lockhead from about 1893 until 1906. He then moved to a firm in Manchester where he was responsible for designing over 100 stained-glass windows.

Mahogany Writing Cabinet

Date: *c* 1903

Designer: **Attributed to George Montague Ellwood (1875–1960)**

Made by: **J S Henry**

The design of this cabinet was previously attributed to W J Neatby, primarily because of the roundels depicting the heads of Art Nouveau maidens. However, a similar piece came to light recently that is clearly marked J S Henry and thus it seems more probable, stylistically, that the designer is George Montague Ellwood, one of Henry's most talented contributors.

Stepped in form, the superstructure has an everted top equalling the width of the base. The upper cupboard is inlaid with roundels of metal and fruitwood, and the designer has let the girl's hair curl outside the boundary of the roundel making the symmetry less formal. The doors house sectioned storage compartments and open to reveal a fall-front writing surface. The base

has a single-frieze drawer and is supported on turned legs united by stretchers. When seen against a wall, the decorative vertical slats break up what would be a dominant open space in relation to the volume of the superstructure. The bold strap-work hinges are interesting without being too elaborate and the piece reflects Henry's interest in the Art Nouveau style.

Bride's Chest

Date: **1905**

Designed and made by: **The Furniture Shop of the Roycrofters (1895–1938)**

Having been so impressed by William Morris when he visited him at Merton Abbey, Elbert Hubbard (1856–1915) bought a small printing press after returning home to America so that he could emulate the Kelmscott Press. In 1896 he founded the Roycrofters, an Arts and Crafts community that produced furniture designs and metalwork. They sold directly through mail order, and Hubbard published two periodicals. He also invited guest lecturers to the community and built a tavern for all those who came to visit.

This bride's chest is made from quarter-sawn oak and the rectangular form is typically plain, complying with the Arts and Crafts 'fitness for purpose' dictum. The upright supports and sides are softened at the top with undulating curves and the keyed tenons are left exposed. The only added adornments are the copper strap-hinges, lock and handles. The name Roycroft, which is carved along the front, and the more often used Roycroft symbol – a double-barred cross and an encircled 'R' – was used as a decorative motif, as well as a means of identification.

Hall Armchair

Date: **1907**

Designers: **Charles Sumner Greene (1868–1957) and Henry Mather Greene (1870–1954)**

Made by: **Peter Hall Manufacturing Co., Pasadena, for the Robert Blacker House, USA**

You only have to look at the design and quality of this teak, oak and leather chair to understand why C R Ashbee was so impressed with American architects Charles Sumner and Henry Mather Greene. Not only is it beautifully made, it is also original and conveys the Greenes' subtle blend of Arts and Crafts and Oriental inspiration.

The Blacker House was designed by the Greenes, with specific woods and motifs for each of the rooms, and was the most overtly Oriental of all the homes they created. The hall furniture was predominantly made of teak, whereas the living room was mostly mahogany.

The back of this chair is gently curved and splayed. The padded leather centre is separated from the uprights by narrow spaces, visually reducing the weight. All the wooden elements have softened edges and the front supports terminate with notched feet.

Other than the configuration of vertical and horizontal elements the most distinctive decorative feature of the chair is the ebony pegs. In some instances they are purely decorative and in others they are a requirement of the construction method. The Greenes and their cabinet-maker, Peter Hall, favoured the Scandinavian slotted screw method of construction, rather than mortice and tenon, because they felt it reduced separation. This method of joinery required that the screws be countersunk and then capped, in this instance, with ebony.

Oak Desk

It may sound fanciful but parts of this architectural-looking desk reflect the Avery Coonley House for which it was made. In particular, the small cupboard doors with raised banding repeat the pairs of casement windows beneath the long, low roof, while the thick writing surface reflects the dominant horizontal line of the building.

The desk has a self-contained feel, and was designed for a guest room in the house Frank Lloyd Wright considered one of his most successful projects. (He also designed the carpets, linen and tableware.)

George Mann Niedecken was a designer in his own right, and president of the Niedecken Walbridge Co., a leading interior design firm. Opinion varies regarding his influence with Lloyd Wright, but it is generally thought that he worked from the architect and designer's drawings. In this instance, the desk's feet are thought to show Niedecken's involvement.

Frank Lloyd Wright was one of the most influential American architects of this century. He conceived that a building, its interior space and the furniture and furnishings that went in it should be considered a whole entity. They should not be separated. He also believed that architecture should be in harmony with its locality, both in style and materials. Unlike his English friend C R Ashbee, he felt that the use of machinery gave both the designer and maker increased opportunities. It was only the unscrupulous use of it by greedy men that caused the problems – not the machine itself.

Date: **1908**

Designers: **Frank Lloyd Wright (1867–1959) and George Mann Niedecken (1878–1945)**

Made for: **Avery Coonley House, Illinois, USA**

Oak Table

Date: *c* 1910

Designer: **Charles P Limbert (1854–1923)**

Made by: **Charles P Limbert Co. (1902–44)**

The perfect balance of this occasional table owes much to the work of furniture designer Gustav Stickley. It has an oval top resting on an X-frame, and plank supports which taper towards the top. The oval under-tier unites the four supports and the cross-stretcher, which is cut out with rectangles. As is often the case with successful furniture design, the blank spaces are as important as the solid forms.

An American, Charles P Limbert sold his furniture under the title of Holland Dutch Arts and Crafts, because it had the right associations with the local Dutch community. His company worked to a high standard and took advantage of machinery, although this was played down in their catalogues.

Desk and Chair

Date: *c* 1907–10

Designer: **Paul Horti (1865–1907)**

Made by: **The Shop of the Crafters, USA (1904–20)**

The idea of the desk as a cabinet on-stand originated in the seventeenth century, but a number of Arts and Crafts designers – notably Charles Robert Ashbee and Charles Rennie Mackintosh – reworked it.

Paul Horti's design is not totally enclosed like a true cabinet, but it does use the fashion for high sides to great effect. The fall-front is recessed and shortened to allow a shelf, and the veneer is cross-banded and centred with an inlaid panel showing a peacock eye. The cupboards on either side are inlaid with a full-length peacock feather, which also enhances the back splat of the chair. Made in mahogany, boxwood, pear wood, mansonia, sycamore and lacewood, the desk has a frieze drawer and is raised on arched block feet united by a board stretcher.

Oscar Onken (1858–1948), who founded The Shop of the Crafters, employed Horti, a Hungarian designer, after seeing his work at the Austro-Hungarian exhibit at the Louisiana Purchase Exposition in 1904. At that time Horti's work was more obviously Secessionist, but he tempered his style to suit the American Arts and Crafts vernacular. These pieces do show the influence of Art Nouveau in the decoration, however.

Pair of Armchairs

Date: *c 1911*

Designers: **William Purcell (1880–1964)**

George Feick Jnr (1881–1945) and

George Elmslie (1871–1952)

These oak chairs were designed for the boardroom of the Merchant Bank of Winona, Minnesota. Their solid appearance looks suitably important, while the plump leather backs and seats suggest success and affluence. The vertical slats break up the surface area, thus creating light and dark and a more dynamic effect.

The rectilinear form is particularly effective at suggesting stability (part of an architect or designer's brief is to reflect the nature of their client's business). The design was then modified, with less sense of authority, for the tellers' and clients' chairs.

Within the architectural partnership, William Purcell created the overall picture for the building; George Feick worked out the precise construction details and George Elmslie unified these in worked-up drawings, which often included decorative details and furniture.

Settle

Date: *c 1912*

Designers: **Leopold Stickley (1869–1957) and**

John George Stickley (1871–1921)

Made by: **L & J G Stickley**

Long and low, this oak and leather settle is 2 m (6½ ft) wide. For comfort it has back and side cushions that fit neatly beneath the inside overhang. When the cushions are removed (as seen here), you can see the fielded panels on the back. The arched supports attached to the front corner uprights are also on the back corners, at right angles to each other, thus making the overhang a useful, rather than a simply decorative, feature. With their curved line, the supports also offer a softer contrast to the sofa's straight and horizontal elements. The extended overhang is a design feature quite often used in Arts and Crafts furniture.

American furniture makers, Leopold and John George Stickley were younger brothers of Arts and Crafts designer, Gustav Stickley. Because they were neither as emotionally or intellectually involved with the Arts and Crafts Movement, they were able to adapt to different styles when the popularity of the Movement started to fade. When Gustav went bankrupt in 1918, Leopold and John George took over his workshops.

Chest of Drawers

Date: **1912–16**

Designer: **Gustav Stickley (1858–1942)**

Made by: **Gustav Stickley's Craftsman Workshops**

(1899–1916)

A major factor in the success of this piece is the use of curly maple, with its soft rippled grain. The top has a broad overhang and a short back rail. The pronounced punctuation of the pulls and the graduated size of the drawers are decorative features in themselves, while the uprights on the edges extend full-length as both frame and support. These are gently bowed and tapered and the nature of the piece would change completely if the uprights were straight.

Gustav Stickley was one of America's most important Arts and Crafts promoters. His pieces were characteristically plain and manufactured to a high standard in his own workshops. In 1903 Stickley hired the architect Harvey Ellis to work for him. Ellis brought a more refined approach, but sadly died the following year. This piece illustrates his subtle legacy – most notably the overhang, the arched apron and decorated band of inlay on the top.

Stationery Cabinet

Date: *c* 1900

Designer: **Ernest Gimson (1864–1919)**

English architect and furniture designer Ernest Gimson made some of the Movement's most beautiful pieces. Together with Ernest and Sydney Barnsley, he revived what was best in English cabinet-making and their legacy may be seen today in the work of the Barnsley Workshops, John Peters and John Makepeace.

This stationery cabinet was made for Gimson's sister, with side doors that enclose the pigeon holes. The front is faced with squares of Macassar ebony veneer, separated by stringing and punctuated by four panels of mother-of-pearl. It is centred with a small door, beautifully decorated with a peacock of inlaid

abalone, mother-of-pearl and lapis lazuli, which encloses a small alcove. The whole piece is supported on chamfered bracket feet. The cabinet is a little gem, dark and discreet in some ways but enlivened by the use of the linear grain and the shimmering qualities of the abalone and mother-of-pearl.

Dining Table

Date: **1916–22**

Designer: **Sir Ambrose Heal (1872–1959)**

Made by: **Heal & Sons, London**

English designer Ambrose Heal must have been pleased with this dining table because he installed one in his own house. The solid, reliable piece is still in the Heals' family home today, and is at its best when laden with food and surrounded by friends and family – all happy, hungry people.

The top, constructed from three chestnut planks with tenoned crosspieces at each end, is raised on solid oak supports. These have chamfered edges on shaped block feet and are united by a plank stretcher. The base and top are fixed by brass plates and the planks are united by butterfly joints. These joints are intentionally left exposed and show the integrity of the construction; they are decorative as well as functional and the piece is in keeping with the principles of 'fitness for purpose'.

A variation on this table was designed by Phillip Tilden for Winston Churchill's house at Chartwell in Kent. In place of the solid square supports, Tilden designed a pair of turned columns, giving a slightly lighter appearance. Churchill liked the refectory-style table because he felt that the narrower width encouraged conversation. Ambrose Heal also liked the variation, and Heal's subsequently reproduced it.

Dining Table

Date: **1923**

Designed and made by: **Sydney Barnsley**

(1865–1926)

This is a classic piece of Arts and Crafts furniture. Designed by Englishman Sydney Barnsley, a major contributor to the Arts and Crafts Movement, the top is made from three planks of English oak. These are united by double-dovetail joints, which are symmetrically arranged for decorative effect. The edge of the table is carved with a lozenge-shaped motif and the frame and supports beneath are angled. The chamfered and angled supports make a huge difference to the table's appearance – it would look so much more pedestrian if it had square legs. Again, the joinery of the dowels and protruding tenons has been left exposed for decorative purposes. The legs are also carved with a vertical repeat of the lozenge motifs.

The master stroke on this piece, however, is the chamfered hay-rake stretcher. This inspired adaptation, taken from a traditional farming tool, was also used by Ernest Gimson. From a visual point of view it works brilliantly, as well as giving the table real strength and stability.

Walnut Wardrobe

Date: **c 1925**

Designer: **Peter van der Waals**

(1870–1937)

This walnut wardrobe shows a cabinet-maker's appreciation of his materials. The figuring of the wood is integral to the success of the piece as it forms most of its decorative effect. Technically, the wood is dead but it glows with such warmth it is hardly surprising that people still consider wood to be the most vibrant medium for furniture – in spite of dozens of modern materials. The raised panels break up what would be broad, plain areas, and allow smaller 'windows' in which the grain can shine. The wardrobe is of framed construction, and the tenons are left exposed on the base.

The skill seen here explains why renowned English craftsman Ernest Gimson employed Peter van der Waals as his foreman cabinet-maker in 1900. After Gimson's death in 1919, the Dutch designer took most of Gimson's workforce with him to new workshops in Chalford, where this wardrobe was made.

Collector's Cabinet

Date: **1928**

Designer: **Sir Gordon Russell (1892–1980)**

Made by: **F Shilton at the Russell Workshops,**

England

This twentieth-century adaptation of a seventeenth-century cabinet on-stand is polished and refined. It was designed by Englishman Gordon Russell and is obviously an important piece, made to commission.

The central display area, with its domed top, gilded interior and sunburst motif above, draws the eye, while the contrasting compartments on either side are darker and less significant.

The walnut cabinet may have been designed to hold a precious piece, for which a worthy backdrop was required. However, it must have been a very special *objet*, not to have been overshadowed by the interior.

The colours and grains of the various woods (including walnut, elm, yew and ebony) are all used to maximum effect, and the ebony feet anchor the piece without being too heavy.

Oak Sideboard

Known as the 'Mouseman', Robert Thompson's sobriquet was coined while working in a church. A fellow craftsman commented that they were both as poor as church mice and, before leaving, the pair carved a mouse on the completed work. From then on, the English furniture maker used the motif as his signature.

The other distinguishing feature of Thompson's work is the adzed finish. If you look closely at the top of this oak sideboard, you will see that it is rippled. This effect is created by using a hoe-like tool called an adze, which is wielded over the wood planks while standing on them. The adze cuts out thin divets of wood and leaves a dappled surface. It takes a great deal of skill to realize a finish as subtle as this, which also affords a stable base, even for wine glasses.

The sideboard's rectangular form and raised back rail is unpretentious and sturdy. It stands on shaped and chamfered legs, and is panelled on the sides, doors and back.

Date: **1934**

Designer: **Robert Thompson of Kilburn**

(1876–1955)

Walnut Armchair

Date: **1943**

Designer: **Eric Sharpe (1888–1966)**

Made at: **Martyr Worthy, England**

One of Eric Sharpe's strengths as a furniture maker was his ability to carve. Here, the back splats of the chair are carved with a repeated scrolling pattern that picks up the line of the head and neck of a swan, which also forms the terminals for the front supports.

As a skilled craftsman, the English furniture maker was inclined to symbolism; this walnut armchair was his wife Marian's favourite piece, and it would be uplifting to think that the swans – known to have only one mate for life – represent his lasting love for her.

Sharpe was also interested in the relationship between the curved and straight line and the patterns produced by the repetition of motifs. Here, he combines straight and curved lines in the chair's form, and connects the stylized carving of the back with the swan heads in the stretcher at the front of the chair. His monogram (in Greek letters) is clearly inlaid on the front.

Jubilee Writing Cabinet

Date: **1977**

Designer: **Edward Barnsley CBE (1900–87)**

Made by: **Barnsley Workshops, Froxfield, England**

Given his eminent forbears (his father was Sydney Barnsley; his uncle Ernest Barnsley), English cabinet-maker Edward Barnsley could be forgiven for turning his back on the family business.

In the early days, Edward produced work like his father's, but gradually developed his own style. He never compromised on the standards set by his illustrious predecessors. As a result, the craftsmanship of this piece is exemplary: the drawers fit perfectly and have Edward's distinctive curved handles which are dished for holding, and the barber-pole inlay and stringing is precise.

Yet another reworking of the cabinet on-stand – this version features a fall-front writing surface. The recessed panels show the craftsman's skilled use of the figuring of the English walnut, and the framing allows us to focus on this.

The Barnsley Workshops still accept commissions. They operate in the traditional way, placing great emphasis on discussions between craftsman and client. The standards set are just as exacting, and an educational trust has been set up to support apprenticeships.

Chapter 2

Art Nouveau

Art Nouveau was a movement which influenced all aspects of decorative art during the last decade of the nineteenth century and the early years of the twentieth. The momentum came from England, where the key figures were John Ruskin and William Morris. They shunned machine-made objects, preferring to substitute their vision of a community of artists dedicated to the revival of creative labour. This brought about a renaissance in handcraft, which in turn inspired the Arts and Crafts Movement. During this time, many guilds and workshops were founded, which had a far-reaching effect on artistic communities in Europe and America.

The global term for Art Nouveau was coined from Samuel Bing's gallery in Paris, called 'L'Art Nouveau', which he opened in 1895. It exhibited the work of innovative artists, and the name emphasized the 'modern' aspects of their pieces. Different countries tended to use their own terminology for the style. In Germany for example, it was called Jugendstil or 'Youth Style'.

Art Nouveau was a linear style, utilizing organic forms as sources of ornament. Nature, symbolizing death, decay and rejuvenation played an important part, as did the influence of Japanese art. 'That Strange Disease', as Walter Crane (1845–1915) called it, was born of a need for new artistic expression, reaching its peak at the Paris Exposition in 1900. By this time, the more

innovative designers had moved on, their work relying as much on geometric principles as on images inspired by nature.

France had two main centres – Paris and Nancy. Furniture from Paris, including work by Georges de Feure and Hector Guimard, tended towards refinement and sophistication. Meanwhile, Nancy, the provincial centre, with work by Emile Gallé and Louis Majorelle, often took its inspiration from its flora, fauna and local culture.

In Belgium, Victor Horta's work – with its whiplash curves – epitomizes what is now considered stereotypical Art Nouveau. The Belgian Henry van der Velde embodied curvilinear vitality in his designs and introduced the Art Nouveau style to Dresden in 1897, while elsewhere in Germany, the work of Peter Behrens, Richard Riemerschmid, August Endell and Bernhard Pankok took a more rectilinear approach to that seen in France and Belgium.

The Wiener Werkstätte in Austria was founded in 1903 by Josef Hoffmann and Koloman Moser with the aim of making and selling the best in modern design and craftsmanship. It adopted a severe but highly functional decorative style, and its work progressed from sinuous linearity to a rectilinear style, taking inspiration from human and plant forms. Charles Rennie Mackintosh was a pioneer of modern design and, together with his Austrian contemporaries, is considered a founder of Modernism.

Yew and American-Maple Dresser

Date: **1897**

Designer: **Richard Riemerschmid (1868–1957)**

Made by: **Wenzel Till, Munich**

One of the best German designers of his generation, Richard Riemerschmid was interested in the relationship between form and function, and this piece combines the simplicity advocated by the Arts and Crafts Movement and the organic feel of Jugendstil.

The cornice with extended overhang is supported on shaped plank sides and square, turned and carved front supports. The apron at the top has a chamfered edge that curves to meet one of the four shelves, and the door, made of American maple, is emboldened by elaborate hinges. The top hinges extend to sinuous tendrils that sweep across the door face, while those at the bottom terminate as small buds.

Riemerschmid's pieces became progressively simpler and more functional, and he was one of the first designers to produce affordable, well-conceived furniture for machine production. He was also a founding member of the Deutscher Werkbund (1907), which played a vital role in bringing designers and manufacturers together in Germany.

Armchair in Padouk

Date: *c* 1899

Designer: **Henry van der Velde (1863–1957)**

With the exception of the front seat support and stretcher, every other element in this chair is curved. Belgian architect and designer Henry van der Velde was influenced by the Arts and Crafts Movement in England and aimed for a structural integrity. Unlike English designers, however, he favoured the curved line inspired by natural images. In a sense, all the individual struts form the frame but their arrangement and the spaces created make up its decorative form. The upholstered seat with its batik cover, designed by the Dutch designer and painter Johan Thorn-Prikker, reflects the curved elements of the chair.

Van der Velde was one of Belgium's most important designers, and his work was particularly influential in Germany. Like a number of other leading figures, he was looking for a rational approach to design which was deeper and more permanent. He wrote frequently on this subject and was appointed director of the newly-created School of Applied Arts in Weimar. He was replaced by Walter Gropius in 1914, and the School evolved into the Bauhaus.

Van der Velde championed artistic creativity over mass production, and his work – simple and organic – exhibits great power. He manages to convey an inner current of strength within the structural elements of his pieces, which can be seen to great effect in his metalwork.

Elm Bookcase

Date: **1899**

Designer: **August Endell (1871–1925)**

Made by: **Wenzel Till, Munich**

German architect and designer August Endell helped to establish Jugendstil in Munich. He also developed his own design theories regarding the applied arts. He came to feel that shapes could be abstracted away from merely copying or representing nature and could be formed as something universally expansive which would affect the psyche. He remarked, 'An entirely new art, the art of using forms that, although they signify nothing, represent nothing, and recall nothing, can move the human soul as profoundly and irresistibly as only the sounds of music have been able to do.'

The top of the bookcase, made by Wenzel Till in Munich, has the fluidity of Jugendstil, while the form is reminiscent of a Hiroshige print. Yet it would be hard to say that these raised motifs were waves, fungi or clouds, although they do make us think of something moving, living or changing. The top edges of the sides are carved but the form is indeterminable, except that it appears to be organic and molten. Aside from these five carved elements the bookcase is very plain, but the shelves act as steps, leading the eye upwards towards the top.

Carved Mahogany Vitrine

Date: *c* 1900

Designer: **Hector Guimard (1867–1942)**

Hector Guimard's work is characterized by an inherent tension, apparent in the structural and decorative elements of this vitrine. This is partly because the French architect and designer looked to branches and stems for inspiration, rather than the more commonly copied buds and flowers.

Nature is seldom symmetrical – a fact which is reflected here. The right-hand upright grows taller to form a partly shaped cornice, and the open, branch-like elements extend to form the horizontal at the top, which in turn merges with the left-hand upright. There is a feeling that certain parts are evolving faster than others, and thus the tension is maintained throughout the piece.

Guimard's most famous commission was for the entrance to the Paris Métro, where his organic wrought-iron structures are entirely appropriate – drawing travellers into the tunnels below.

Lacquered Beechwood Cabinet

Date: *c* 1908

Designer: **Attributed to Otto Prutscher (1880–1949)**

Otto Prutscher, an Austrian architect and designer, had various teaching posts in Vienna and was also involved in a number of municipal construction projects. He was a principal designer at the Wiener Werkstätte along with Josef Hoffmann and Koloman Moser, and his integration of form and decoration is illustrated in this piece, which is restrained and sophisticated.

Although it is black-lacquered, the solid form is saved from appearing too heavy by its rod-like legs, which feature carved additions of formalized flowers and foliage. The two doors are inlaid with polished pewter, which flows with wave-like fluidity over the side panels flanking the glazed central section – and punctuated with spots of mother-of-pearl that contrast with the lacquer. The vitrine has a simplicity epitomized by Oriental pieces, which is broken by a classical Greek key pattern in the top section.

Walnut and Fruitwood Sideboard

Date: *c* 1900

Designer: **Jacques Gruber (1870–1936)**

The glass panels in this sideboard were a regular feature of French designer Jacques Gruber's work. Here, the glass depicting branches of fruiting cherry is acid-etched to reveal the yellow beneath the red. The panels are divided by wooden struts and imitate the way stained glass is often segmented.

The sideboard is effectively framed by boldly carved verticals and an arched top, with the fruit motif carved in the shaped panels on either side of the central bank of drawers. The drawers themselves have subtly-carved fielded panels.

Gruber was a professor at the School of Decorative Arts in Nancy, and this walnut and fruitwood sideboard is an excellent representation of the School's style of Art Nouveau.

'The Enchanted Princesses' Cabinet

Designed at the turn of the century, this cabinet was ahead of its time. It shows Koloman Moser's knowledge of Japanese art, and his skill as a graphic artist. The Austrian painter and designer's choice in using the Princesses as his subject conveys strong romantic symbolism.

The inside of each door shows a female figure in marquetry, adorned with an inlaid metal crown. Her long hair envelops her body and she appears to 'float' in a stream of inlaid alpacca 'bubbles' of varying sizes. These figures may easily have been inspired by Wagner's Rhine maidens.

The friezes above and below are carved with highly formalized water lilies and waves, illustrating the influence of Japanese graphic arts in their two-dimensional form.

When the doors are closed, you can see six asymmetrical glass water drops. The metal lock plate is embossed with stylized fish and bubbles, continuing the aquatic theme. The cabinet is of triangular section, raised on three broad plank-like supports with alpacca metal sabots. The simple rectilinear form represented a modern style appropriate for the new century.

Date: *c* 1900

Designer: **Koloman Moser (1868–1928)**

Made by: **Portois & Fix, Vienna**

Mahogany Wardrobe

Date: *c* 1900

Designer: **Georges de Feure (1868–1928)**

Art Nouveau can be incredibly elaborate or, as can be seen here, quite restrained. The pediment with its softened line is carved with stylized flowers on the corners and a sinuous plant motif in the centre. The central doors are flanked by two smaller cupboards, enclosing drawers and shelves which, in turn, are divided by another small drawer. Each of the fielded panels has rounded corners and the base and feet are carved with plant motifs. The 'nature' theme is carried through to the brass handles, which are cast as ears of wheat, with 'whiskers' forming the hinged pulls.

A similar piece to this was shown at Samuel Bing's Pavilion 'Art Nouveau Bing', at the Paris Exposition in 1900, for which Georges de Feure, a French artist and designer, received critical acclaim.

Serving Table

Date: *c* 1900

Designer: **Gustave Serrurier-Bovy (1858–1910)**

As an architect, the Belgian Gustave Serrurier-Bovy took great care with the interiors of his rooms. They were usually colourful, with walls and ceilings decorated in stained glass, wood panelling and faïence fireplaces.

Although his work is clearly Art Nouveau, one can see the restraint exercised by the influence of the Arts and Crafts Movement. (Serrurier-Bovy was greatly impressed by William Morris, and showed a bookcase at the Arts and Crafts Exhibition Society in 1896.)

The serving table, which was designed for the Paris Exposition in 1900, is an interesting combination of curved and straight lines. The undulating top rail, with its linear horseshoe band, intersects with the shaped shelf and faïence-tiled back. The base is rectangular, but has an arched apron and stretcher beneath it. To complete, the designer combined the lock plates and hooped handles in hand-beaten copper, having centred them with coloured enamel, a favoured device.

Two-Seat Canapé and Chairs

Date: *c* 1900

Designer: **Edouard Colonna (1862–1948)**

Edouard Colonna was a talented jewellery, porcelain and furniture designer and his work is characterized by an attractive delicacy and lightness of form. He also worked for Samuel Bing, and exhibited a drawing room at the Paris Exposition in 1900 to great critical acclaim.

The mahogany frame is of fluid outline, carved with sinuous ribbon detailing. The armrests terminate with scrolls, and the legs are tapered and slightly upturned at the front. The embroidered Oriental silk (new) is upholstered in panels to emphasize the asymmetry of the design. (The combination of Art Nouveau and Oriental would be appropriate for the period.)

The length of the back and the arched sides of the canapé and chairs are a distinctive feature and add to the suite's graceful appearance. It would be particularly suitable for a large drawing room, where the backs of the chairs could be easily viewed.

Pear Wood Lady's Armchair

Date: *c* 1900

Designer: **Hendrik Berlage (1836–1934)**

Made by: **t'Binnenhuis, Holland**

Hendrik Berlage was one of Holland's most influential architects. He advocated a more rational approach to design, as illustrated by this eminently practical chair. The angled back and the upholstery add comfort, but the decorative qualities lie in the arrangement of the structural elements.

There was a strong socialist ethic behind Berlage's work. An early Modernist, he felt that good, functional design should be available to all, and that the machine was the best way to achieve this. It is interesting how one man's socialist view should be so different to another's. William Morris also wanted to deliver good design to the masses, but he was unable to achieve his aim because he rejected machinery and the drudgery it brought.

Hanging Cabinet

Date: *c* 1900

Designer: **Jean-Auguste Dampt (1854–1947)**

A trained sculptor, Jean-Auguste Dampt also designed lighting, jewellery and medals. His furniture output was small because he made everything by hand. This fair-sized piece is 1.96 m (6 ft 5 in) high and 1.12 m (3 ft 8 in) wide, and used to hang on the wall of the French designer's studio in Montmartre.

The frame and structural elements of the cabinet are made in oak; the back is of burr walnut. Each of the verticals is carved with stylized foliate motifs. The varying levels and depths make the piece more visually interesting, and the carved finials elongate and lighten the heavier central section. The oval motifs at the very bottom are sensitively carved, blending with the burr walnut almost as if they are a part of the wood.

Ash and Bird's-Eye Maple Buffet

Date: *c* 1900

Designer: **Eugène Gaillard (1862–1933)**

Eugène Gaillard was another of Samuel Bing's protégés. The French designer showed a piece like this at the 1900 Paris Exposition, only the applied decoration on the glazed doors was of cast bronze, rather than wood. The piece was bought from Bing's Pavilion by the Museum of Decorative Arts in Copenhagen.

To Gaillard, the frame was important in unifying the various elements. He also felt that furniture should suit its purpose and highlight the qualities of the materials used. With this buffet, the frame grows up from four feet to merge into the sinuous pediment. Thus, the centre and its flanking shelves and cupboards are brought together. The carving on the cupboards and glazed doors is incredibly fluid and demonstrates the surprising plasticity of wood in the hands of a skilled craftsman.

Lady's Desk

Date: **1900**

Designer: **Bernhard Pankok (1872–1943)**

Made by: **United Workshops, Munich**

Bernhard Pankok was a graphic artist and painter before turning to furniture. As a furniture designer he had a very individual style that evolved over the years. Jugendstil, like Art Nouveau, was inspired by nature, and this mahogany and cherry wood desk draws its inspiration from the insect world.

The segmented form of the desk is similar to an insect's body, with the separate top drawer, the shelf beneath this and below the desk top, the angled back and the three obviously separate drawers. In addition, the broad sweep of the back is divided like wings, coloured and patterned like a moth.

The legs are of curved form and those at the front are tapered and carved with foliage that entwines itself like a climbing plant, adhering to the surface, growing stronger and higher.

Walnut Armchair

Date: *c 1901*

Designer: **Josef Urban (1872–1933)**

In this simple but effective design Josef Urban combines the chair's back, sides and front legs to form a continuous sweep that terminates with brass sabots on each of the tapered supports. The stylized Scottish rose on the side shows the impact of Charles Rennie Mackintosh, whose work had been shown the previous year in Vienna. The seat is plain and the vertical splats at the base of the back break up the surface area.

An Austrian designer, Urban went on to achieve fame in America, where he was well known as a theatrical designer. He was the architect for one of the Ziegfeld theatres and designed sets for a number of Broadway shows. He also designed sets for over 20 Hollywood films and became head of stage design for the Metropolitan Opera House in New York.

Carved Walnut Screen

Date: *c* **1901**

Designer: **Johan Thorn-Prikker (1868–1932)**

Made by: **J C Altorf**

Nieuwe Kunst in Holland was broadly divided between those who followed the functional approach of Berlage and those who favoured a more obviously decorative art. Dutch architect, furniture and textile designer Johan Thorn-Prikker falls into the latter category. An admirer of Henry van der Velde, his work was usually more organic than this piece, which was designed, together with a crib, for his patron, Dr Leuring, to commemorate the birth of his first child.

The crib and this three-fold screen are shown together in a contemporary photograph, and although the decorative motifs are different they follow a circular theme. The sides of the cot are lower than the screen's inlaid panels, so that visually they do not compete. The cot sides are decorated in open work, with ammonites framed as graduated circles. The screen panels are inlaid in ivory with circular motifs like floating bubbles, and the carved iguanas at the top are not bold enough to frighten a child.

Tea Table

Date: **c 1901**

Designer: **Pierre Selmersheim (1869–1941)**

Made by: **Asseur**

Like all good Art Nouveau furniture, this piece has a tensile strength to it that is tangible in the supports. The organic qualities are integral to its form and are not applied. The eight carved arms that form the centre of the piece each support a circular tray, similar to the stems and leaves of lily pads. The top tray is upheld on three supports above a lower tier raised on spindles. This is then connected to the satellite trays by a central hoop. All of these elements are linked by a main stem that terminates in a bud where the legs unite. The four legs end in feet that resemble elegant wooden clogs.

For all his artistry, the French designer has not lost sight of his purpose – the mahogany tea table is functional as well as stylish.

Small Jewellery Cabinet

Date: *c* 1901

Designer: **Joseph Olbrich (1867–1908)**

Made by: **Robert Macco, Heidelberg**

Joseph Olbrich was one of the leaders of progressive Viennese architecture. He was a founding member of the Secession, and designed their new exhibition in 1897. Two years later, with five other designers, the Austrian was invited by Grand Duke Ernst Ludwig of Hesse to Darmstadt in Germany to form an artists' colony and prepare for an exhibition called A Document of German Art.

Olbrich introduced Darmstadt to the Viennese geometric forms and decoration – a style he learnt during his time as assistant to Otto Wagner. He designed almost all the buildings within the colony, including the central studio and exhibition hall. As a special commission he also built a furnished child-sized house for the Grand Duke's daughter, Princess Elisabeth, in the grounds of Schloss Wolfsgarten.

This small jewellery cabinet is appropriately gem-like. Its tapering rectangular form is made from stained maple, and the twin doors, secured with large silvered copper hinges, are inlaid with stylized ivory flowers with abalone shell centres. The side panels are similarly decorated, and the interior is lined with silk.

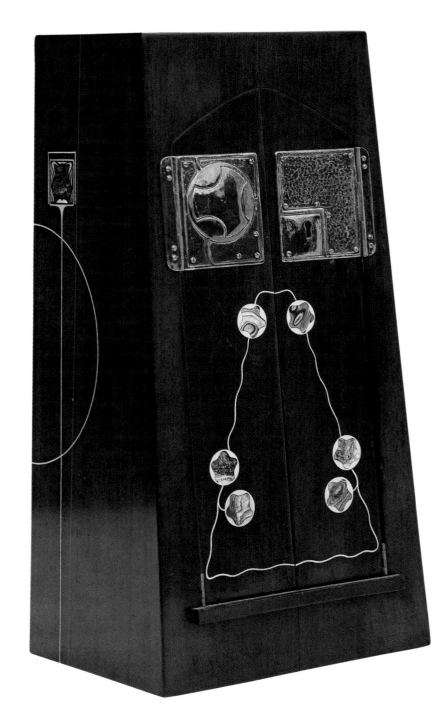

Stained Beech Dining Chairs

Date: **1902**

Designer: **Peter Behrens (1868–1940)**

Peter Behrens was one of Germany's most influential figures. He was involved with the Munich School and the artists' colony in Darmstadt, and also taught in Dusseldorf, Berlin and Vienna. He became the artistic adviser to the giant German electrical company AEG, and designed buildings and domestic appliances for them. At one time Mies van der Rohe, Walter Gropius and Le Corbusier all worked for him.

These chairs were designed when Behrens was in Darmstadt and have a strong linear presence. The form is softened by the curved uprights and lightened by the spaces created by the positions of the vertical and horizontal elements. Each element is left as a separate entity, which, when united, forms the chair. The top rail with its pierced oblong centre is stepped higher than the central supports and the central splat is clearly locked into it. Raised on waisted supports united by pairs of stretchers, the chairs have drop-in woven cane seats enclosed by a deep apron.

Carved Padouk Armchair

One of the most organic of all the turn-of-the-century designers, Antonio Gaudí's buildings, metalwork and furniture look as if they have, quite literally, grown from roots in the ground.

The Spanish architect's influences were varied. He took inspiration from the French Neo-Gothic Movement of Viollet-le-Duc, as well as Art Nouveau, John Ruskin and Moorish architecture. Combine these with his Catalonian heritage and the result is fantastically original work.

This chair is so 'alive' one almost expects it to start walking. Perhaps this is because the elements have such human characteristics, including the heart-shaped back and its spine-like support, the curved arms with their biform terminals, and the legs with their knee-like protrusions and bulbous feet.

Date: *c* 1902

Designer: **Antonio Gaudí y Cornet (1852–1926)**

Vellum-Covered Chair

The name Bugatti immediately conjures up images of burning rubber, but that was Ettore Bugatti, the car designer; this is Carlo, his father.

Carlo started his cabinet-making business in 1888, and is the best-known Italian designer from the turn of the century. His style was eccentric and original, with an acknowledgement to Art Nouveau in his use of motifs taken from nature.

Bugatti's design for the Turin International Exposition of 1902 was awe-inspiring. He created four innovative rooms, and this chair comes from *Salle de Jeu et Conversation*, latterly known as The Snails Room due to its resemblance to the interior of a snail's shell. The cavernous chamber was entered through a small arch, where this chair and three others were grouped.

The chair is made of wood and looks as though it has grown naturally, rather than having been constructed. The circular back rest has an embossed copper panel, and the skilled application of the vellum defies belief. The surface is painted in gold, red and black, and depicts highly formalized insects and plant forms.

Date: *c* 1902

Designer: **Carlo Bugatti (1856–1940)**

Desk Chair

Date: **1902**

Designer: **Bruno Paul (1874–1968)**

Made by: **Vereinigte Werkstätten,**

Munich

The most striking features of this ash wood chair are the strong fluid lines and the distinctive back supports, which make additional ornamentation unnecessary. The curving sweep of the back and arms is emphasized by the cut of the grain. The front supports are tapered on the inside of the legs, and the V-shaped back splats channel the weight down to each rear leg. The arms of this chair, designed for use at a desk, dip towards the front supports in order not to compete with the edge of the desk top.

The strong fluid lines and lack of ornamentation are typical of the German designer's work at this time. Bruno Paul helped to foster a revival of Arts and Crafts in Munich, and was a founder of the Vereinigte Werkstätten für Kunst im Handwerk, where this chair was made. Later, his work became more rectilinear. He was a founder of the Deutscher Werkbund and later designed very successfully for mass production.

'Orchidée' Carved Desk

This mahogany desk was designed by Frenchman Louis Majorelle, who was considered by critics the 'undisputed master' of Art Nouveau furniture design. Majorelle, a contemporary of Emile Gallé from the Lorraine district of France, combined superb design with the finest technical virtuosity. His woodwork was astonishing, producing sculpturally fluid lines one could only believe possible in a more malleable material.

The practical working surface has a fluid outline, with gilt-bronze banding above an apron inlaid with lighter-coloured wood, giving the impression of burr wood. Accommodated within the apron is a long drawer and two shorter ones, with gilt-bronze handles of floral inspiration.

The piece is supported on four slender legs, with sculptural vertical fluting. The hoof-like sabots that extend at the front terminate in heart-shaped panels, enclosing a flower. The mounts on the back legs extend further to become electric lamps in the shape of orchids. The lamps' organically conceived shades were fashioned by the Daum Brothers' glass studios in Nancy.

Date: *c* 1903

Designer: **Louis Majorelle (1859–1926)**

Ebonized Oak Writing Cabinet

Date: **1904**

Designer: **Charles Rennie Mackintosh (1868–1928)**

Made by: **Alex Martin**

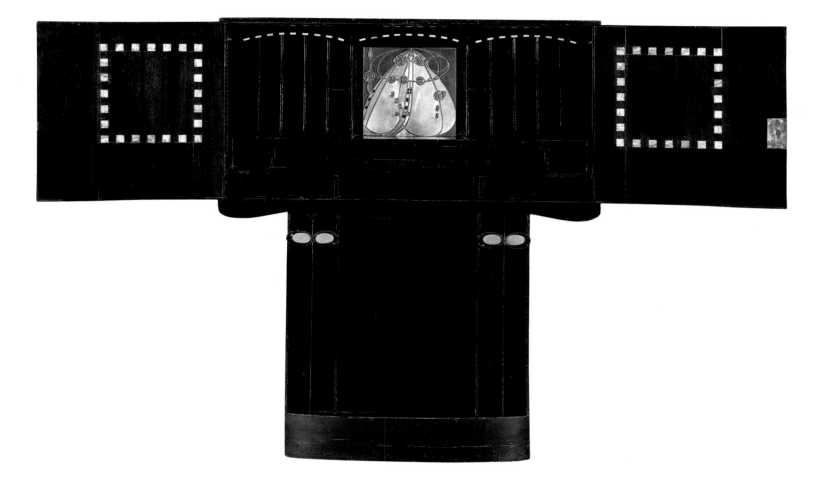

This fabulous oak writing cabinet was the single most expensive piece of furniture Scottish architect and designer Charles Rennie Mackintosh ever designed. It cost £22 0s 6d and was made for Walter W Blackie of Hill House. In recent years, it has become the most expensive piece of twentieth-century furniture sold at auction.

The sturdy, ebonized wooden structure has doors set with panels of mother-of-pearl squares above an ogee apron. The doors open to reveal a fitted interior, and a central leaded-glass panel, probably designed by Mackintosh's wife, Margaret MacDonald. The panel features Glasgow-school 'rose-balls' with inlaid ivory above three arches, resembling eyebrows.

When it is open, the cabinet resembles a hanging Kimono, and reflects the influence of Japanese art.

The inner doors are strikingly punctuated with further squares of mother-of-pearl.

Sadly, Mackintosh was only appreciated by a few in his lifetime. However, he was fortunate enough to have the patronage of Walter Blackie, for whom he created Hill House, the largest and most finely detailed of his domestic commissions. It is the only one of his houses that retains much of the original interior.

Chair in Bent Beech and Wicker, Model No. 2

Date: *c* 1904

Designed and made by: **Gebruder Thonet, Vienna**

Michael Thonet was originally granted exclusive rights to make his bentwood furniture in 1842. The bending was effected through the agency of steam or boiling liquids. After the patent expired in 1869, many firms jumped on the bandwagon. All were eager to copy the light, versatile styles wrought by the Austrian furniture designer's revolutionary techniques.

Gebruder Thonet, as the company became known from 1852, won medals at the Great Exhibition in London in 1851, and at the Paris Expositions of 1855 and 1867. The company merged with their competitors Mundus J & J Kohn in 1932, and expanded their range to also include bent tubular steel furniture.

Characterized by lightness and versatility, the bentwood chair, in all its variations, is one of the great success stories in the history of furniture. They have been an integral part of twentieth-century living, and there can be few people in the Western world who have not sat in one. What would the cafés of Paris have done without them?

Elbow Chair

Date: **1904**

Designer: **Charles Rennie Mackintosh (1868–1928)**

Made for: **Hous'hill, Glasgow, Scotland**

This elegant chair was designed for the drawing room of Miss Kate Cranston's home, Hous'hill, in Glasgow, and shows great sophistication. The tall back tapers slightly and has a severe horizontal top. The back splats are punctuated with mauve glass plaques, reflecting those in a screen to which this chair originally stood adjacent. Unusually, the splats extend to ground level, their cross-sections changing direction on their downward journey. The elegant arms slope forward and their cross-section changes from square to flattened.Below a padded drop-in seat, the apron is arched.

The redoubtable Miss Cranston was an active supporter of the Temperance Movement and owned a number of tearooms in Glasgow. According to the journal, *The Builder*, Glasgow was a 'veritable Tokio for tea rooms', and Mackintosh was regularly called upon by Miss Cranston to exercise his design skills for the benefit of Glasgow's tea lovers.

'Aube et Crépuscule' Bed

Date: **1904**

Designer: **Emile Gallé (1846–1904)**

It is sadly ironic that this fabulous bed should have been ordered to celebrate a marriage, while simultaneously heralding the forthcoming death of its creator. The bed was commissioned by Henri Hirsch, along with a magnificent vitrine that was supported on the back of monumental dragonflies. As the name suggests, the bed symbolizes the beginning and end of the day and the eternal circle of life – death, decay and rejuvenation – depicted in stunning marquetry.

The headboard represents twilight, with a pastoral scene that was probably inspired by Lorraine, the French designer's homeland. The exotic woods remain unstained and speckled with tiny fragments of mother-of-pearl, resembling stars, which reveal a shepherd and his flock beneath the vast wings of a moth.

Dawn is symbolized on the footboard, and shows a pair of confronting butterflies, their wings beautifully carved in shallow relief and inlaid with mother-of-pearl mosaic. The butterflies flank an opal-like carved glass cabochon, reserved against a ground of more butterflies, the panels held within sinuously fluted frames.

Collector's Cabinet and Vitrine

Date: *c* 1905

Designer: **Leon Jallot (1874–1967)**

Leon Jallot was the head of Samuel Bing's atelier, before opening his own studio in 1903. His own style was more conservative than the lavish designs promoted by Bing's gallery, as is clearly illustrated here. It probably also explains why the French cabinet-maker was one of the few designers to make a successful transition to Art Deco.

The rectangular form, with reeded uprights, has a pediment carved with stylized flowers alternating with applied bronze moths. The dappled grain of the burr walnut, seen to great effect on the doors, also acts as a wonderful backdrop to the glass shelves. Below this is a carved frieze of stylized flowers and leaves, which are repeated on the pediment and roundels. These roundels are centred with bronze moths that have cleverly disguised loop pulls across their backs.

Mahogany Sideboard

Date: *c* 1905

Designer: **Eugene Vallin (1836–1922)**

Having served an apprenticeship at his uncle's cabinet-making factory and studied modelling at the School of Design in Nancy, French architect and furniture designer Eugene Vallin's early work was in the Gothic style, inspired by Viollet-le-Duc. However, his transition from Gothic to Art Nouveau was a swift one.

This sideboard is taken from a truly spectacular dining-room suite, which also includes a dining table and twelve chairs, a serving table, a pair of console tables and a chandelier. As with all good Art Nouveau pieces, the outer frame of the sideboard has a tensile strength and fluid line. The arched and trifid supports that unite the superstructure at the front with the base are an innovative adaptation of Gothic flying buttress, and the play of light on the fluted and carved surfaces adds to the sense of energy and growth. The carved figures appear as playful putti, introducing a benign presence which does not upset the overall balance.

Silver, Enamelled and Stone-Set Vitrine

Date: **1908**

Designer: **Josef Hoffmann (1870–1956) and**

Carl Otto Czeschka (1878–1960)

This vitrine is as much a huge jewel as it is a functional piece of furniture. Made by craftsmen at the Wiener Werkstätte and displayed in 1908 at the Kunstschau, Vienna, it is the product of a wonderful collaboration between Austrian architect Josef Hoffmann and decorative arts designer Carl Otto Czeschka. Hoffmann probably supplied the architectural structure of the piece with its interesting fenestration and Czeschka, a recognized graphic artist, the strong illustrative quality of the figures and detail.

The borrowings from nature are evident, with pierced images of exotic birds, squirrels and a mouse amid foliage set with mother-of-pearl and bunches of baroque pearl 'fruits'. There are five barbed oval windows on each side, above which a shaped onyx top is held aloft by a pair of caryatic figures with carved ivory faces and hands. The figures wear Secessionist garb with oval floral motifs punctuated with blue enamelling, their chequered sleeves in two-coloured mother-of-pearl and elaborate head-dresses set with lapis lazuli. The whole rests on a walnut parquetry base.

The piece has the quality of a medieval reliquary and delights the eye, while at the same time keeping a foothold in the twentieth century.

Beech Cabinet

Eduard Josef Wimmer was an important member of the Wiener Werkstätte, joining in 1907 through his involvement with the decoration of the Cabaret Fledermaus and becoming one of Josef Hoffmann's closest associates. He successfully directed the fashion department of the Wiener Werkstätte following its formation in 1910, and latterly taught at the Art Institute of Chicago for two years.

Wimmer's involvement with textiles, fashion accessories, graphics and wall coverings can be seen in his stimulating use of geometric forms and materials in this cabinet. His personal style was close to what we now call Art Deco, and the stepped architectural form of the cabinet anticipates, by more than a decade, the skyscrapers of New York in the 1920s.

The eye is drawn towards the top in increments, the storage space on each level appearing to diminish behind fewer or smaller doors – their almost lozenge-shaped ebony motifs contrasting against the golden beechwood. The mitred arrangement of each linear panel on the doors creates an optical illusion, in the same way as some patchwork quilts do. Each tier is beautifully banded in mother-of-pearl.

Date: *c* 1913

Designer: **Eduard Josef Wimmer (1882–1961)**

Bentwood Two-Seater Banquette and Chair

Date: *c* 1916

Designer: **Attributed to Gustav Siegel (1880–1970)**

Made by: **J & J Kohn, Austria**

Jacob and Josef Kohn, a father and son partnership, began their business as timber merchants, but graduated to making furniture. Like a number of other companies, they saw the opportunity to join the growing market for bentwood furniture. Gebruder Thonet were leaders in the field having held an exclusive patent until 1869. When the patent was up, Mundus J & J Kohn started copying Thonet designs (along with many others). In 1899 they appointed a young designer called Gustav Siegel to run their design department and his youthful vigour and talent took them ahead of the pack.

Kohn also had the foresight to commission some of the leading members of the Vienna Secession, notably Otto Wagner, Josef Hoffmann and Adolf Loos. They offered simpler, but visually striking furniture in contrast to the excessively scrolled designs of the previous century.

Unfortunately, most of the design records for Kohn after 1900 have been lost or destroyed, so it is difficult to accurately attribute some designs. This suite has also been attributed to Hoffmann and Koloman Moser, but the most recent academic arguments favour Gustav Siegel.

Mahogany Sideboard

Date: **1916**

Designer: **Michel (Sam) de Klerk (1884–1923)**

Made by: **t'Woonhuys, Amsterdam**

Michel de Klerk, a Dutch architect and furniture designer, was one of the leading proponents of what became known as the Amsterdam School, along with Piet Kramer and J M van der Mey. At its height between 1915 and 1921, the School reacted against Berlage's functionalism, and was developed as a form of expressionism. In terms of furniture, this meant that 'function', the original driving force, was replaced by the imagination and creativity of the artist.

This sideboard, along with the rest of the sitting room, was designed for t'Woonhuys and was illustrated in their furniture catalogue in 1919. The theme of the room, including wall hangings, carpets and colour scheme, was based on marine subjects. Thus, the armrests on the chairs terminated with fish heads, and the hinges have been inspired by angel fish. The most interesting design feature is the central bank of drawers, around which the doors close. The long ebonized handles, which terminate with aquatic foliate motifs in wrought iron, pull open to leave the drawers open and exposed.

Black Stained Oak Dining Chair

Date: *c* **1917**

Designer: **Hildebrand Lucien Krop (1884–1970)**

Made by: **Nusink & Son, Amsterdam**

A member of the Amsterdam School, 'Hildo' Krop was a prominent Dutch sculptor, who also designed furniture. This chair is from a dining-room set and is a very distinctive variation on the traditional ladder back.

The three elements that form the frame of the back are joined by the domed horizontal splats which stand proud at the rear and are themselves united by oval beads. Marjan Groot points out in her essay on the Amsterdam School that they are similar to a ribcage joined by the spine.

The tapering uprights, which are broad and rounded, extend down to form the legs and terminate with oval feet. In turn, these are united to the front supports by a deep, angled side apron. The chair is completed by the drop-in seat, covered in red velvet for added drama. This chair, made by Nusink & Son in Amsterdam, is bold, robust and confident of the space it occupies.

Chapter 3

Modernism

The Arts and Crafts Movement left historicism behind in favour of simpler, more functional forms. They praised the craftsman's skill, championed the applied arts and developed the idea that the design skills of artists and architects could be used for interiors. True, in Europe, they shunned the machine, but a vital step had been made – the cleaner style of 'fitness for purpose' made the progression towards Modernism and Mies van der Rohe's principle of 'less means more' much easier and understandable.

Stylistically, shortly after the turn of the century, designers like Charles Rennie Mackintosh, Josef Hoffmann and Frank Lloyd Wright were all creating more geometric and abstracted designs.

The decade between 1910 and 1920 was a time of great artistic evolution. In the applied arts the machine began to be considered as the way forward. Radical developments were occurring in the fine arts and the barriers between them and the applied arts had been broken down during the previous century. Pablo Picasso and Georges Braque were painting in the abstracted Cubist style, and the Italian Futurists were concentrating on engineering and technology – the new idioms of the century.

In Russia there were the Constructivists whose dictum was minimal geometric themes, and in the Netherlands the De Stijl group consisted of a band of artists and

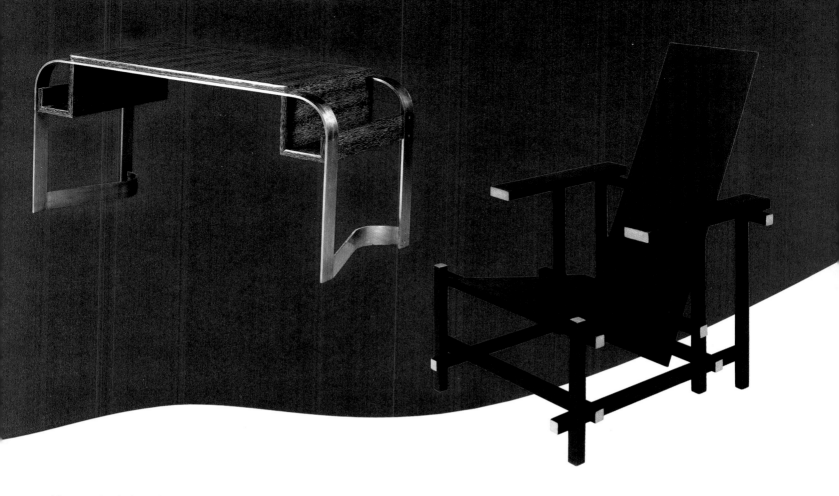

architects who believed in pure abstraction to geometric shapes, and the use of primary colours in addition to black, white and grey.

Following along similar lines, Charles Édouard Jeanneret (more commonly known as Le Corbusier) and Amedee Ozenfont developed their theories of Purism, again based on the universal qualities of pure geometric shapes. New materials with different properties had a great impact on the designs of the period and, like all movements, it lost its rigid adherence to the original rules over time, becoming more rational rather than purely functional. This period also saw the birth of modular (or unit) furniture.

In 1907 the Deutscher Werkbund was formed in a bid to bring German artists and manufacturers together. The belief was that items that were well designed and made would be more likely to sell. The machine and mass production was a vital ingredient in this equation, and the opportunity to exploit foreign markets prompted other countries to establish their own versions of the Werkbund. The British variant,

for example, was called the Design Industries Association.

The Bauhaus fitted into this scheme perfectly. Founded by Walter Gropius in 1919 the original aim of the German school was to unify the traditional skills of craftsmanship with new technology in order to produce innovative designers. Gradually, however, the syllabus changed. Over time, the Bauhaus became a school of modern design and technology, aiming to produce pure and simple designs that would be available to all, thanks to the economic assistance of machines.

The Modernists aimed to design furniture with pure lines and a geometric form that could be easily mass produced. Pieces should be without decoration, as the form would say it all. At its best, Modernism has created some design classics that are still in production some 70 years after their conception. At its worst, it produced furniture that was bleak, sterile and inhospitable.

Rood Blauwe Stoel (Red/Blue Chair)

A classic of the Modern Movement, the Red/Blue chair is the epitome of De Stijl design, with its flat rectangular planes and horizontal and vertical frame. The frame elements are either of square or rectangular section, emphasized by yellow ends. All the pieces seem separate, but connected by a central core like a skeleton; here, the spine is the flat, angled back and seat.

This is design pared down to its bare minimum. It could easily be mass produced, and maybe even assembled at home.

The prototype for this chair was made from plain wood. Dutch architect and furniture designer Gerrit Rietveld brought it to life by using the primary colours advocated by Piet Mondrian and Theo van Doesburg, the De Stijl group's painters. The open spaces combined with the structural elements give the chair a sculptural, assured quality.

Date: **1918**

Designer: **Gerrit Thomas Rietveld (1888–1964)**

Made by: **G van de Groenekan**

Upholstered Armchair

Date: **1920**

Designer: **Walter Gropius (1883–1969)**

Made by: **Tecta Mobel, Germany**

Architect, designer and founder of the Bauhaus, Walter Gropius felt that the interior and furnishings of a building – as well as the building itself – should be linked, and that every architectural project should proceed with this in mind. He also felt that every object – chair, desk, vase – had an 'essence' which was derived from its function and its limitations. Careful research of this, combined with new materials and technology, had the potential to produce some unusual and surprising designs.

A pair of these chairs and an accompanying sofa were first designed in 1923 for the director's room at the Bauhaus in Weimar. Supporting the geometric principles behind Modernism, the German designer put furniture that was based on squares, cubes or rectangles into a square room.

Even the furniture that was rectangular looks as if it could be sub-divided by cubes or squares.

Originally, the chair was made in cherry wood and the upholstery was of lemon-coloured wool cloth. Later versions have been made in different colours, including one in monochrome, and the black base, through the illusion of painting out, makes the seat appear unsupported.

'EF 928' Bed

Date: **1925**

Designer: **Pierre Chareau (1883–1950)**

French architect and designer Pierre Chareau was very interested in the idea of incorporating movement into conventionally static pieces of furniture. As a result, many of his designs have an adjustable or articulated feature, and although the furniture itself may not be moveable, a part of it will be.

This wrought-iron suspension bed attaches to the wall at the back and is supported at the front on tubular steel uprights that are fixed to the floor. The spring base and mattress are suspended by steel rods, and the frame at the top allows the bed to move. The bed is simple and refined, and next to a white wall it has a stark and elegant clarity.

Chareau was one of the most innovative of all the Modernist designers. His versatility – from pure Modernism to Art Deco – is quite amazing. His work was mostly commissioned by private clients, rather than aimed at mass production.

Wassily Armchair

Date: **1925**

Designer: **Marcel Breuer (1902–81)**

Made by: **Gavina, Milan**

Apparently, Marcel Breuer, a Hungarian architect and designer, took his inspiration for this chair from a bicycle. With the aid of a local plumber, who helped him to weld the tubular frame together, he eventually achieved the finished product. He was keen that it was made on the production line at a bicycle factory, but no one would oblige him.

Again, the chair is based on the cube; the main frame and supports look as if they are made of one single bent piece of chromium-plated tubing, although they are not. This sense of fluidity adds to the overall light and airy feel of the chair, while strength and tension is achieved by the taut, slingback seat and rests.

Marcel Breuer was one of the finest students to come out of the Bauhaus, and this design is one of the most enduring tubular metal and leather chairs in production.

Writing Table in Sycamore

Date: **1926**

Designer: **Pierre Chareau (1883–1950)**

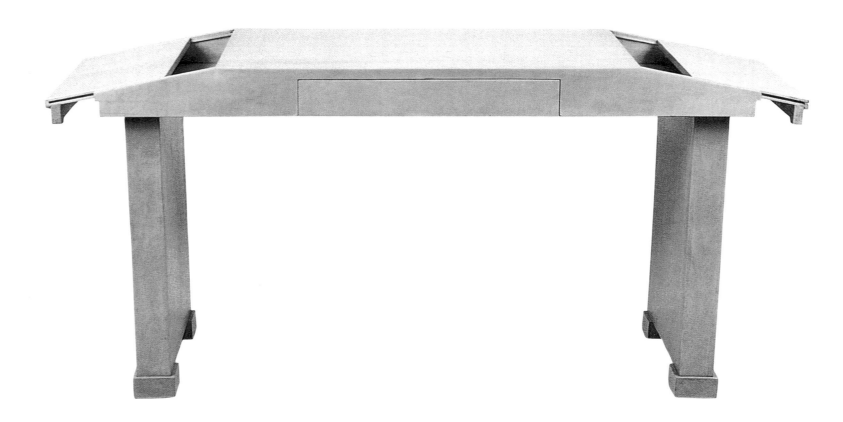

It is over 70 years since this table was designed and yet it still looks fresh. The proportions of the top and the weight of the supports are perfectly balanced; the edges are finely rounded to take away unnecessary sharpness and the frieze drawer and slide-covered compartments fit flush, making the whole piece appear sleek and elegant.

It was suggested that the angled sliding sides were impractical because objects could not be placed on them. This is true, but French designer Pierre Chareau did not design the table to have things piled upon it. It is a table for writing letters on, which can then be put away in one of the compartments. The writer can reach for another sheet of paper or a bottle of ink without moving or having to adjust his chair.

Chareau was a very innovative designer, who straddled the line between Modernism and Art Deco. He eschewed ornamentation but was not without innovation. He preferred designing for individuals rather than for the masses.

Cantilevered Chair

Date: **1926**

Designer: **Mart Stam (1899–1986)**

Made by: **Thonet**

When Mart Stam designed this chair he believed that the function of an object should be the sole determinant of its design. He also believed that, where possible, mass production should be the method of manufacture. According to Stam, aesthetics were not an issue. 'Away with the furniture artists,' he once said, requiring that chairs need only be comfortable to sit in and easy to move around.

This chair is very unassuming because it has been reduced to a point where it occupies very little space. The tubular metal is bent and turned in one fluid piece, to be joined at the back of the floor support. The cantilever is possible because of the strength and spring of the metal.

A Dutch architect and town planner, Stam did not design a great deal of furniture, although he did produce a variation of this chair with arms.

Bar Table

Date: *c* 1928

Designer: **Paul Dupré-Lafon (1900–71)**

There seems to be very little biographical information about French interior designer Paul Dupré-Lafon. He worked for a small group of wealthy clients, shunning the Salons and the exposure they offered. Presumably, his reputation was spread by word of mouth, as his furniture was designed specifically for clients' needs, rather than for mass production.

This table is very angular and compact. The geometric form is enlivened by the way the angles and planes relate to one another, and there is no added ornamentation. The rectangular top has a storage well which has been enclosed by a hinged cover edged in nickel-plated bronze. This is a practical consideration for a table such as this, taking into account the knocks it would receive. The nickel-plated base is of triangular shape, repeating the form of the front upright edge. At one end there is a cupboard with a long hinge that Dupré-Lafon chose to leave exposed rather than conceal.

Chaise Longue

Date: **1928**

Designers: **Le Corbusier (Charles Édouard Jeanneret) (1887–1965), Pierre Jeanneret (1896–1967) and Charlotte Perriand (1903–99)**

Made by: **Cassina (since 1965)**

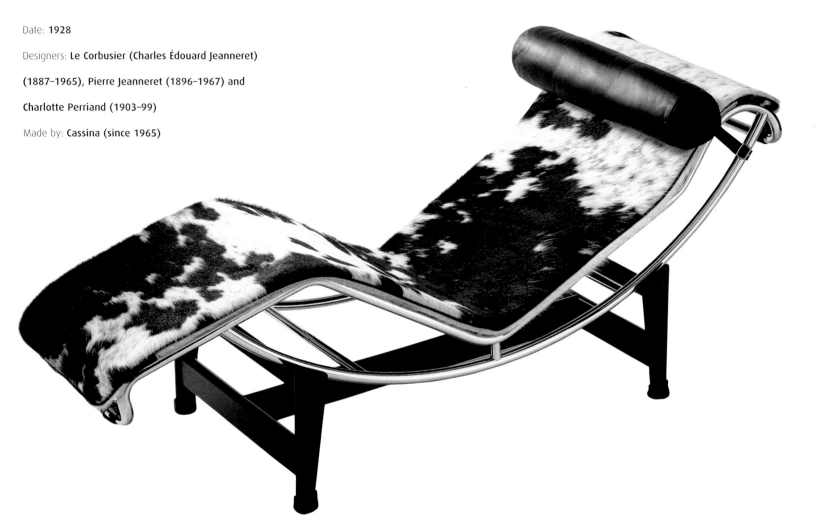

This flexible chaise longue enables the user to recline at any angle he or she desires. You can stretch out on a flat horizontal, have your head or your feet raised, or take the chaise off the base and rock in it. Its shape was ergonomically designed to fit the human body,

and the fact that it is still selling successfully testifies to its comfort and enduring design quality.

The undulating tubular-steel frame sits on the base and the broad open spaces beneath it create the feeling that the chaise is 'floating on air'.

Le Corbusier, a Swiss architect and designer, was one of the most influential twentieth-century architect designers. For this piece he collaborated with his cousin Pierre Jeanneret and French furniture designer Charlotte Perriand to produce a twentieth-century classic.

Sheet-Steel Chair

Date: *c* 1928

Designer: **René Prou (1889–1947)**

Made by: **Labor Metal**

At first glance, it is not obvious that this chair is made of sheet steel. The black paint and plump upholstered seat distract us from the metal used – a material not usually associated with a comfy chair. French architect and designer René Prou had worked extensively with wood, but began working in metal towards the end of the 1920s.

Other designers were also experimenting with tubular steel, but the seats and backs of their furniture were always made of a softer material such as canvas, leather or cane. Very few were brave enough to let the metal come in direct contact with the body.

The pattern for this chair started from a single sheet of metal. Skilled workers had to roll the top rail, fold the edges and rests, and weld in the seat. The cut-out sides reduce the visual weight as well as the physical, and remind us of designer Gerald Summers, who worked from a single sheet of plywood (p. 109).

Macassar Ebony Desk

Date: **1929**

Designer: **Donald Deskey (1894–1989)**

Donald Deskey was a leading American designer, most famous for the interior of Radio City Music Hall in New York. His design background included architecture, engineering and painting. He studied in France and attended the 1925 Paris Exposition, visited the Bauhaus and was interested in the work of the De Stijl group. In European terms, his work is difficult to categorize, as he seems to straddle both Modernism and Art Deco.

The architectural form of this desk is dramatic. Its stark clarity is emphasized by the contrasting darkness of the Macassar ebony and the reflective nature of the brass. Similarly, the skeletal open-metal support contrasts with the solidity of the semicircular drum, while the linear grain of the ebony emphasizes the vertical and horizontal elements of the desk.

Barcelona Chair, MR90

Date: **1929**

Designer: **Ludwig Mies van der Rohe (1886–1969)**

Made by: **Knoll**

One of the most significant architects of the twentieth-century, Ludwig Mies van der Rohe also left his mark on furniture design.

The German designer started out as an apprentice to Bruno Paul. He later worked for Peter Behrens, and took over the directorship of the Bauhaus in 1930. In 1937 he moved to America to escape Nazi Germany.

This is a supremely elegant chair. From the side, it consists of two sweeping lines that cross each other. Buttoned leather cushions (not shown) are supported by straps attached to horizontal bars which unite the two sides. The chair was expensive because it was hand-built, and Mies modified the joints when Knoll started to produce it in stainless steel in 1948.

The X-frame has been used as a chair support for centuries. Mies's interpretation of it was so successful that the Barcelona chair is still in production today.

Dressing Table

Norman Bel Geddes was a prodigious American talent. He was a successful theatrical designer before turning to industrial design. In 1932 he wrote a book called *Horizons*, in which he proposed the tear drop as the ideal streamlined shape.

By nature metal is cold, hard and not immediately acceptable to people looking for comfortable home furnishings. However, it became more popular over time and, up to a point, streamlined steel became a symbol of modern, efficient America.

Here, Bel Geddes has used enamel on metal in the same way as Art Deco designers were using lacquer on wood. This, combined with the rounded edges of the dressing table, produces a sleeker look. It is also much cheaper than lacquer on wood. The shiny surface of the enamel and the reflective qualities of the chromium plating and mirror add to the sense of light and sophistication.

Date: **1929–32**

Designer: **Norman Bel Geddes (1893–1958)**

Plywood Armchair

Date: **1930**

Designer: **El Lissitzky (1890–1941)**

Made by: **Tecta (D61)**

This inexpensive chair was designed for the Hygiene Exhibition in Dresden. It is a simple variant of the tub chair, made principally from a single sheet of plywood that is painted so that it can be easily cleaned. The arms and seat are screwed into place and are plain except for their shape; the different elements are emphasized by different colours.

Due to his travels in Europe, Russian architect and designer El Lissitzky was familiar with all the major groups of the Modern Movement. He taught at the Vkhutemas Moscow Design Institute – the Soviet version of the Bauhaus – and was perhaps most influential as a graphic and typographical designer.

Pair of Skyscraper Bookcases

Date: **c 1930**

Designer: **Paul T Frankl (1887–1958)**

American designer Paul T Frankl was born in Austria and trained there while the Vienna Secession was at its height. However, he felt that each country developed its own style and America and the Modern Movement was no exception. As a result, he fully embraced the culture of his new home, and used the stepped form of the skyscraper as a source of inspiration.

The bookcases, with their linear emphasis and plain flat surfaces, seem to rise upwards without support. The black background gives the effect of painting out and allows the red edges and shiny metal rods to appear to float effortlessly in space.

The bookcases are functional, but the arrangement of the shelves is not uniform. One of the horizontal planes extends beyond the boundaries of its own form, and the metal rods as an outside edge are really unusual. Think how different they would appear if the tubular metal was changed to the same red edge. The rods almost act as a thread piercing the horizontal planes and uniting them.

Japanese Oak Corner Desk

Date: **1930**

Designer: **Sir Ambrose Heal (1872–1959)**

Made by: **Heal & Sons, London**

Heal & Sons was originally founded in 1810 as a feather-dressing firm. Under the leadership of Ambrose Heal, it grew into a world-renowned furniture and furnishings company. In 1913 Heal & Sons moved to a new building in Tottenham Court Road, London, where the floor-to-ceiling windows allowed customers to view products in natural light.

The Mansard Gallery on the top floor was used to promote in-house design, as well as contemporary art.

In 1919 you could have bought a Modigliani for 2s 6d; in the 1930s, furniture by Mies van der Rohe, Marcel Breuer and Alvar Alto was also available.

This architectural desk, with concealed handles, is made from quarter-sawn Japanese oak. The weathered effect was created using a wire brush to deepen the grain. This was filled with Plaster of Paris, and the surface was sanded down when it was dry. The highlighted grain was then finished with wax.

Heal & Sons survived the Second World War and exhibited at the Britain Can Make It Exhibition in 1946, featuring designs by Christopher Heal, Robert Heritage and A J Milne. The company backed Robin Day's and Clive Latimer's Leaning Storage System, which won first place in the 'Low Cost' competition at the Museum of Modern Art in New York in 1948; through the 1950s and 1960s the pair could do no wrong.

Games Table

Date: **c 1930**

Designer: **Charlotte Perriand (1903–99)**

This avant-garde table fits our expectations of furniture in the twenty-first century rather than the early twentieth. Its square top, with circular ashtrays at each corner framed by square chromium-plated plaques, is raised on intersecting metal sheets. Each chromium-plated surface reflects the support at right angles to itself, giving an impression of being able to see beyond the table. The supports are set on the angle, so players can sit with their legs unimpeded.

Charlotte Perriand was a radical French interior and furniture designer. In 1927 she exhibited a bar interior at the Salon d'Automne. The furniture was made from chromium plate and anodized aluminium, and its futuristic appearance was shocking to many. Le Corbusier, however, was impressed. He hired Perriand, who collaborated with him and his cousin Pierre Jeanneret from 1927–37.

Art historians believe that Perriand triggered Le Corbusier's involvement with metal furniture, helping to produce several pieces that have subsequently become twentieth-century classics.

Paimio Chair

Date: *c* **1930**

Designer: **Alvar Aalto (1898–1976)**

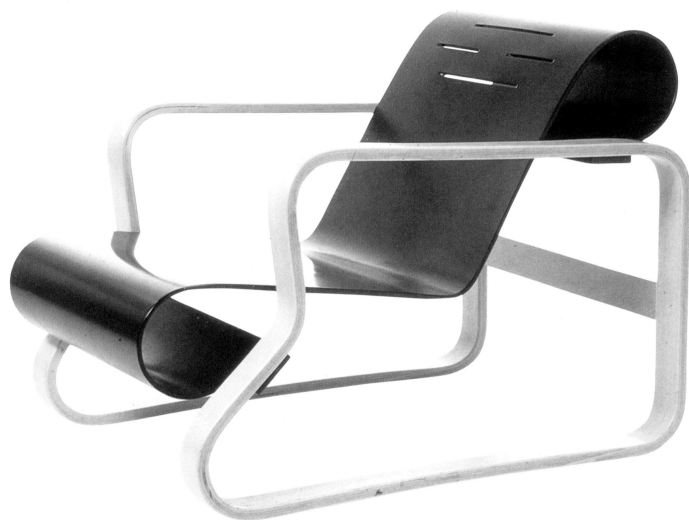

Alvar Aalto considered furniture to be the extension of a building. As a result, when the Finnish architect designed the Paimio Tuberculosis Sanatorium in the 1930s, this chair was designed specifically for it.

Conscious that his furniture was to be used by seriously ill patients, Aalto rejected the trend for tubular steel. Although it was hygienic and easy to move, he felt it failed the patient. 'Tubular and chromium surfaces are good solutions technically, but psychophysically these materials are not good for the human being,' he wrote. Instead, he used laminated birch plywood, which he felt fit both criteria.

Together with the furniture technician Otto Korhomen, Aalto spent many years exploring ways to mould and produce laminated wood efficiently and economically. The Paimio chair is a perfect illustration of this. The scrolled back and seat are made from a single sheet of laminated birch plywood and the supports and rests from laminated birch. The form is beautifully fluid, and the curves of the open frame are soft and approachable.

Coffee Table

Date: *c 1930*

Designer: **Denham Maclaren (1903–89)**

The thick glass top of this coffee table is upheld on three elliptical supports. These are united by S-shaped tubular-steel rods, which are also visible through the top. The rods are of an interesting configuration and only connect to the supports on one side, although British designer Denham Maclaren emphasizes the fact that the rods pierce the supports by capping the ends and leaving the metal exposed. It is as if we are seeing some formalized mechanism through a glass.

Sadly, Maclaren gave up designing at the end of the 1930s. The strong, clean lines, shiny metal and dense black-lacquered wood of this coffee table, combined, with Maclaren's dramatic use of glass, make the designer's limited output regrettable.

Mahogany Sideboard

Date: **1930**

Designer: **Kaare Klint (1885–1954)**

Made by: **Rudolf Rusmussens Snedkerier,**

Copenhagen

Mass production and standardization go hand in hand, and Kaare Klint was one of the first designers to study the needs of people before creating a product. The Danish designer studied which items people put into what cupboards and planned drawers and shelves accordingly. The size and design of this sideboard was determined by the nature of the items it was to store.

He reduces the visual weight of the sideboard by raising it on a stand. Otherwise, it is of plain rectangular form with rounded edges. The sliding doors have fielded panels with recessed handles and carrying handles have been added to facilitate moving. The two slide shelves in the base are a practical addition, allowing items to be sorted here, rather than on the floor.

Driven by a rational approach, Klint took his aesthetic inspiration from Oriental, Shaker and eighteenth-century English pieces.

Coffee Table

Date: *c* 1930

Designer: **Anonymous, probably Italian**

Made in laminated birch, lead and glass, this Futurist table is like a giant mechanical component. The interacting segments are reminiscent of cogs, and the glass top is symbolic of the wheel. In fact, the whole table looks as if it is in a state of motion, or about to be.

The Futurists believed art and design should reflect the innovations of the modern age – trains, planes and automobiles – not past achievements. This table is made of multiple abstracted shapes that are built to different levels. The highest part is capped with lead and the groove cut into its side secures the glass, allowing the cantilever to work and the table to be safe.

Tubular Chair

Date: **1930**

Designers: **Wassili Luckhardt (1889–1972)**
and Hans Luckhardt (1890–1954)

Made by: **Thonet**

This plywood and tubular-steel chair was created by German designers Wassili and Hans Luckhardt, and has moved on from the cube as the basis of its form. It still has the properties of lightness, practicality and economic viability, but the curved outline makes it more streamlined.

Steel played a large part in the Modern Movement. It transformed architecture, and its strength and flexibility offered great possibilities for furniture design. In addition, chromium plating was perfected as a commercially viable process by 1925, and its non-tarnishing properties were a perfect partner for steel.

In 1931 Hans Luckhardt wrote: 'Steel furniture is a living expression of our striving for rhythm, functionality, hygiene, cleanliness, lightness and simplicity of form. Steel is the material that is hard, resistant, durable, but which, at the same time, flexibly responds to the free creative urge.'

Metal and Glass Bed

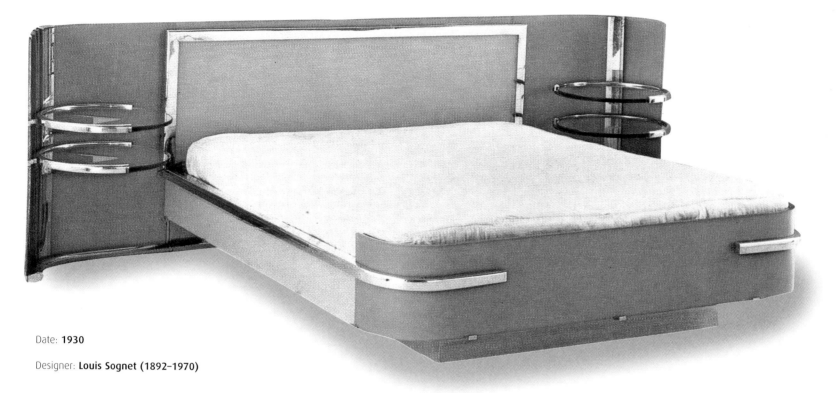

Date: **1930**

Designer: **Louis Sognet (1892–1970)**

This bed was bought in France to furnish the Maharajah Yeshuant Rao Holkar's new palace in India, which was built by German architect Eckart Muthesuis.

The bed is made of glass and chromium-plated metal, which are easy to maintain. In addition, both materials are comparatively cool to the touch – a vital consideration for designing furniture in a hot climate. The *eau-de-nil* colour of the glass was very popular at the time, and reflects the renewed interest in Egypt following the discovery of Tutankhamen's tomb.

The bed is functional and plain, but Louis Sognet's use of materials makes it striking. The chrome is used for dramatic effect, but also protects the glass edges where they are most vulnerable. The two tonnes of glass used by the French cabinet-maker and furniture designer emphasize the different elements, while the raised platform creates the impression that the mattress is floating.

Dressing Table

Date: **1931**

Designer: **Robert Mallet-Stevens (1886–1945)**

This sycamore and aluminium dressing table strips away our preconceptions of furniture and form. It is well equipped with a broad, practical top, an adjustable mirror, a drawer, cupboards and plenty of shelf space – all of which have been left unenclosed.

The exposure emphasizes the table's formal geometry and plain surfaces, making it a perfect example of Modernism. However, the spaces created by the French designer also make the piece fun and 'user-friendly'. The openness of the table reduces any sense of self-containment and pretension; one could make – and look – a mess here, and not feel reproach.

Aluminium Chaise

Date: **1932**

Designer: **Marcel Breuer (1902–81)**

Probably made by: **Enbru Werke, Switzerland**

The Modernists were very keen to exploit new technology and materials because it released them from historical precedents. The means to extract aluminium had been around since 1886, and chromium since 1798, but it was the munitions industry of the First World War that brought them to commercial development. The aeroplane and automobile industries saw the potential of aluminium as a strong but light metal – and the glues that had been developed for an earlier era of flight were to prove a great asset in the development of laminates.

Marcel Breuer's functional approach has produced a light, comfortable and visually distinctive chaise. The profile of the chair is in keeping with the human form, and was first produced in aluminium in 1932. Later, when the Hungarian architect and designer lived in England, he adapted the design for Isokon, a plywood furniture firm.

Palm Wood Desk

Date: *c 1932*

Designer: **Eugène Printz (1889–1948)**

Eugène Printz has used two contrasting materials for this desk to create a bold and simple form that is both powerful and elegant. The distinctive linear grain of the palm wood top is in keeping with the desk's rectilinear form. This contrasts with the reflective surface of the wrought iron with its pronounced curved line. Printz said: 'I admire the seductive harmony between the straight lines and the curves, and this originality which is at one and the same time daring and discreet.'

Printz, a Frenchman, was an apprentice in his father's cabinet-making business, which specialized in French reproduction furniture. It was not until 1925 that he struck out with his own designs, and began to establish his reputation and a very select clientele.

Dressing Cabinet

Date: **1932**

Designer: **Eileen Gray (1879–1976)**

Eileen Gray was one of the most original artists of the period – modern, innovative and unpredictable. She did not design for mass production, and retired before the Second World War, leaving a small but distinctive body of work.

Gray designed two houses with the technical aid of Jean Badovici. The first was E-1027 in Monte Carlo, and the second her home, Tempe a Pailla, also in the South of France. During the process she became very involved with specific storage needs, investigating what people really needed for their homes.

The rectangular form of this dressing cabinet is made of oak and cork, the latter being a material favoured by Gray for its 'quietness'. When placed against a wall, the spaces will be filled by its colour and the shelving will act as its frame. The door and drawers have no applied handles, just cut-out holes. This cabinet came from her home, but she had designed a similar one for the house in Monte Carlo in aluminium with mirrored doors.

Tubular-Steel Desk

Date: **1933**

Designer: **Wells Coates (1895–1958)**

Made by: **PEL**

This desk was made by PEL (Practical Equipment Ltd) a company formed in 1931 by a group of manufacturers of tubular steel, who wished to capitalize on the surge of interest in tubular-steel furniture.

Oliver Barnard was PEL's artistic director, but guest designers also contributed, including British architect and designer Wells Coates. This desk owes much to Marcel Breuer, who designed a similar piece for Thonet in 1929.

As a pedestal desk, it has two banks of graduated drawers, but differs from conventional form with the open space/shelf that separates the top from the drawers. The contrast of chromium and black emphasizes the different elements, but only really looks good if the condition of the surfaces is rigorously maintained. The desk is extremely functional and was well-suited for the purposes of mass production.

Plywood Armchair

Date: **1933-4**

Designer: **Gerald Summers (1899–1967)**

Made by: **Makers of Simple Furniture, London**

This has to be one of the best examples of an economic use of materials, ever. Take a single sheet of plywood, make four incisions and cut away a small section. Mould and bend the wood, and you have a modern, simple and fluid chair.

Sadly, however, this brilliant design by English designer Gerald Summers wasn't particularly easy to make; as a result it was unable to compete price-wise with its Scandinavian competitors.

The cream-tinted chair was originally designed for overseas markets. The single-sheet plywood form was ideal for tropical climates where traditionally jointed furniture was subject to separation. It could be used without upholstery, which is susceptible to rot in humid conditions, as well as being a habitat for insects.

Chest of Drawers

Date: **1933**

Designer: **Gilbert Rohde (1894–1944)**

Made by: **Herman Miller, Michigan**

This chest of drawers is simple and refined. Its decorative content is derived from the rectangular form and the use of materials. Interestingly, the graduated drawers are veneered in English sycamore, but rather than cover each drawer with its own sheet, American designer Gilbert Rohde chose to unite them by splitting the veneer and dividing it between the drawers.

He also used two types of wood with different grains and colours to emphasize the various elements. The darker sucupiro wood forms the top, the asymmetrically placed handles and the feet.

'Airline' Armchair

Date: **1934**

Designer: **Kem Weber (1889–1963)**

Made by: **Airline Chair Co., Los Angeles**

The streamlined furniture designs of 1930s' America were closely identified with the aerodynamic theories that transformed the shapes of cars and aeroplanes. Streamlining became the epitome of Modernism and is well illustrated by American designer Kem Weber's chair. He has set out to design a chair that by its very form looks as if it has been created by speed.

The chair was designed to be light and easily transportable – something that could be sold for home assembly. The main feature of the design is its cantilever; the side struts give extra strength to the frame through applied pressure when someone sits in the chair. The stretchers that unite the sides are fitted together with self-tightening joints.

'Nocturne' Radio, Model No. 1186

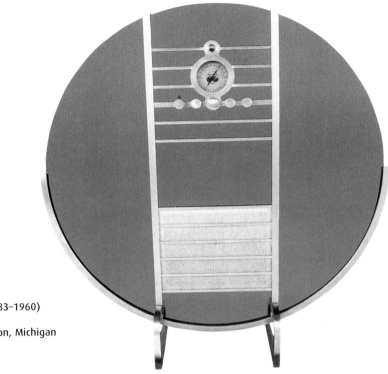

Date: *c* 1935

Designer: **Walter Dorwin Teague (1883–1960)**

Made by: **Sparton Corporation, Jackson, Michigan**

The radio was a major invention of the twentieth century; by the 1930s there was one in every home. As far as designers were concerned, it was a very exciting product as there was no historical design precedent.

A radio or wireless in the 1930s had the same status in a room as a television has today. Radio cases were items of furniture as transistors had not yet been invented. This one stands at 1.16 m (3 ft 9½ in) high, 1.10 m (3 ft 7½ in) wide and 39 cm (15½ in) deep and was designed by one of America's most prominent designers. The blue glass face is supported by a metal frame and divided by vertical and horizontal lines, the effect of which is very striking.

Chaise Longue

Date: **1936**

Designer: **René Herbst (1891–1982)**

René Herbst was one of France's leading Modernist designers. The architect and designer enjoyed working with metal and exploring the opportunities that new materials presented.

In the case of this chaise longue, the strength of the tubular steel allows the designer to produce a long, low structure without the need for additional legs in the centre. The seat and back have a wooden frame covered with rattan, and because it follows the contours of the base, the back looks as if it has been peeled away from it and set at a 45-degree angle. It appears languid and surprisingly fluid for stark and functional Modernism.

Herbst was among a collection of avant-garde designers who broke away from the more conservative Société des Artistes Décorateurs. The new group included Charlotte Perriand, Pierre Chareau and Jean Prouvé among its members, and was called the Union des Artistes Modernes. They staged their first exhibition in 1930.

Occasional Table

Date: *c* 1939

Designer: **Archibald Taylor (1900–75)**

This table is a perfect example of technology inspiring design. It was created for the home of Robert Scanlon in San Francisco, and designer Archibald Taylor used a turbine for the base. The glass top is fixed to the base with a metal cap and raised on four splayed supports.

The main feature is the stylized use of the truncated blades of a rotary engine. Their angled position reflects light and shadow and each blade is aerodynamically tapered on one edge. The blades' circumference is set perfectly in line with the glass.

If you were to draw a line from the edge of the top down to the base and then up to the other edge, you would complete a semicircle. This brings harmony to a piece of furniture that might otherwise be ungainly.

Aluminium Armchair

Date: **1942**

Designer: **Gerrit Rietveld (1888–1964)**

Made by: **Gerrit and Wim Rietveld**

It is right and fitting that this chapter should end with Gerrit Rietveld – the designer who began it. The creation of this chair can only be viewed as a spontaneous act by an innovative designer in unusual circumstances.

Apparently, the Dutchman found the aluminium for this chair at the crash site of a British plane during the Second World War. Together with his son, he salvaged the metal and proceeded to fashion the chair using a corner of his kitchen table to puncture the holes. By folding the metal, the designer made optimum use of the single sheet, and reduced the need to add too many extra pieces. The back legs were added, however, in addition to the struts which have been riveted between the sides and the seat to prevent the chair from collapsing when someone sits on it. All in all, it is the ultimate in recycled furniture.

Chapter 4

Art Deco

Art Deco was born at much the same time as Modernism, with many of the same events impacting on its development. Cubism, Post-Impressionism, the Futurists and the Fauves all helped to forge Art Deco, as did the spectacular Ballets Russes. Later, one could add the discovery of Tutankhamen's tomb in 1922 and the stepped Mayan temples of Mexico.

As with Modernism, the emphasis was on the geometric, but the difference lay in craftsmanship. Art Deco utilized traditional cabinet-making skills, which resulted in its exponents being branded as elitist by the Modernists, as only the rich could afford such labour-intensive pieces.

A vacuum had been left in France following the demise of Art Nouveau and it took a while for a new style to emerge. The French had been impressed by an exhibition of Munich designers, including work by Richard Riemerschmid in 1910. Their work showed an integrated interior of fine and applied arts, but was aimed at a wide audience and the pieces were machine-made to a high standard. As a result, a few French designers started down the Modernist route. Others took the idea of the integrated interior and the harmony it accorded but used traditional craft skills added to the geometric style of the day.

One of the main proponents of this was the architect André

Vera who thought the French should take inspiration from the last true style of Louis XIV, and should mix it with twentieth-century simplicity and eighteenth-century motifs. This time, however, the motifs would be flowering and fruiting baskets and swags – as opposed to the traditional flaming torch and bow and arrow.

The 1925 Paris Exposition Internationale des Arts Décoratifs et Industriels Moderne is seen as the pivotal point when the French style, later known as Art Deco, was shown to the world. The exhibition had been due to take place in 1912 but was postponed.

American designers had been invited to exhibit at the Exposition but they declined, feeling they had nothing 'modern' to show. Afterwards, however, a touring exhibition visited various American museums, and department stores staged their own exhibitions, each bringing the new style to the American public. This prompted an American search for their own new style and,

like the Futurists, they were inspired by machines, automobiles and aeroplanes. Designs were geometric, but the essential American ingredient was streamlining.

Science and technology were impacting on design. Thanks to aerodynamics, automobiles and aeroplanes were streamlined, so why couldn't other objects be designed accordingly? Electricity was now available in virtually every home; radios were the new phenomena and the revolution in domestic appliances was an exciting growth area. Add to this the skyscraper, and you have the multiplicity of American Art Deco.

Unlike the Modernists, the proponents of Art Deco were not afraid of decoration. They worked with abstraction but were not devoted to pure geometry; neither were they seeking innovation with man-made materials, preferring to use materials, such as ivory and sharkskin, found in old colonial Europe.

Sofa

Date: **1913**

Designer: **Josef Gočár (1880–1945)**

Made by: **Prague Artistic Workshop**

Inspired by the Cubists, Czech architect and designer Josef Gočár designed this stained-oak sofa for a well-known actor called Otto Boleska. Gočár was a member of the group of avant-garde artists who were influenced by Cubism before the First World War, and which also included architects and sculptors.

Today, this piece would be characterized as Art Deco, with its zigzag back and flat angular planes. However, the date of the design shows that the Movement started earlier than the 1920s–30s, which are the decades more usually associated with Art Deco pieces.

With regard to the zigzag, it is interesting to see Gočár's use of the motif in a stepped, graduated progression. Firstly, in the wooden back, then the back with its padded, tapered panels at counterpoint, and lastly the seat and wooden apron, again at counterpoint, and at a much wider angle.

Giraffe Cabinet

Date: **1915**

Designer: **Roger Fry (1866–1934)**

Made by: **J J Kallenborn & Sons, London**

Roger Fry, an English designer, set up the Omega Workshops in 1913 with a group of artist friends. Decoration rather than form was the primary objective, and furniture was bought second-hand purely for the purpose of painting it. They had no special craft ideals in the way that William Morris did and pieces such as this – albeit designed by Roger Fry – were made by a cabinet-maker outside the Omega Workshops.

To further facilitate creative freedom, none of the pieces were individually signed. Instead, they bore the Omega stamp, thus removing expectation of a specific artist and fostering experimentation.

The marquetry technique suits the semi-Cubist style. Here, the geometric shapes are effective in the various coloured and grained woods, particularly the striped wood of the giraffes. The geometric background is continued on the back of the shelves, which are stepped and graduated, perpetuating an appropriate sense of elongation.

Amboyna Encoignure

Date: **1916**

Designer: **Jacques-Emile Ruhlmann (1879–1933)**

This is a classic example of the flowering motif that the architect André Vera was advocating as a feature of the new French style. This exquisite corner cabinet is inlaid with ebony and ivory and the work is so fine that it allows very close scrutiny. Considered one of the finest furniture makers of the twentieth century, Jacques-Emile Ruhlmann follows a tradition of previous French masters.

The cabinet is of triangular form. The slightly bowed front is made in amboyna with ivory inlay to punctuate and unite the various elements. There are dentilated plaques of ivory at the front edge, inlaid dots on the perimeter of the doors, and ivory sabots and scrolls. We are also treated to a magnificent display of ebony and ivory in the centre. There are several versions of this encoignure in different woods, and each is equally impressive.

Canoe Sofa

Date: **1919**

Designer: **Eileen Gray (1879–1976)**

This elegant sofa reflects an interest in exotic cultures at the time, and is thought to be based on a Polynesian canoe. Its Irish (later French) designer Eileen Gray learnt the art of lacquer from a Japanese master called Sugawara. The refined lacquer finish looks like melted chocolate, and contrasts richly with the silver leaf of the interior.

It is not known who the sofa was made for, but it is similar to one Gray made for Madame Matthieu Levy. (There is a wonderful photograph of her reclining on it, with silks draped over the side.) The low sweeping form is interrupted only by the undulating edge and the arched supports. The use of silver on the interior gives an opulent, slightly decadent feel, but the nature of the silver leaf softens the overall effect, making it subtle rather than garish.

Fire Screen

Date: **1921**

Designer: **Jean Goulden (1878–1947)**

Made by: **Jean Dunand**

The vibrancy and depth of colour in this fire screen show why lacquer became such a fashionable medium in the 1920s. It also testifies to the expertise of Swiss lacquer artist Jean Dunand who executed it. During that time, there were comparatively few artists skilled enough to produce such fine work.

The plain black frame and supports blend unobtrusively with the background to show a scene of moonlit cypress trees and a farmhouse depicted in eggshell. Dunand executed the screen based on a drawing by his friend, French painter and designer Jean Goulden, and a panel of the same design was exhibited at the Galerie Georges Petit in 1921.

Dunand and Goulden, along with Paul Jouve and Francois Louis Schmied, formed an artistic association and exhibited collaborative and individual works together on a regular basis at the Galerie Georges Petit. Because their work complemented each other, the exhibitions proved successful and continued until 1933.

Lit-Soleil

Date: *c* 1930

Designer: **Jacques-Emile Ruhlmann (1879–1933)**

If you want spectacular Art Deco, then you need look no further than the work of Jacques-Emile Ruhlmann.

This piece is dramatic, thanks to its bold shape and precise use of veneer. The strong linear grain of the Macassar ebony is focused at a central point and radiates out through the concentric circles. The colour contrast within the wood is its own decoration, and Ruhlmann has enhanced it by focusing our attention and framing and controlling the fine burst of lines. The sides, feet and footboard are simple, with rounded edges for comfort. There are no ornate embellishments; the wood is left to speak for itself.

The French furniture maker only used the best materials, and his pieces were executed to such high standards that only the very wealthy could afford them. He justified this by saying that the patronage of the rich would elicit the best of modern design, which could then be interpreted for the benefit of all.

L'age D'or

Date: *c* 1923

Designers: **Edgar Brandt (1880–1960) and**

Max Blondat (1879–1926)

This magnificent wrought-iron screen confirms Edgar Brandt as the pre-eminent ironsmith of the 1920s and 1930s. His early work also included Art Nouveau-style jewellery, and he exhibited regularly at the Paris Salons from 1905.

In 1919 Brandt established his own atelier, employing the latest technology and gaining important commissions, including the fabulous ocean liner *Normandie*. He opened his showrooms in London and New York under the name of Ferrobrandt, and collaborated with the architects of the Porte d'Honneur at the 1925 Expositions Internationale in Paris. He also designed his own exhibition pavilion and the ironwork for the pavilions of Jacques-Emile Ruhlmann and René Lalique.

Here, we see evidence of his partnership with French sculptor Max Blondat, whose architectural background enabled him to design on a large scale.

Each of the three vertical panels is centred with an octagonal beaded plaque, enclosing a man and a woman flanking The Three Graces, in gilded bronze.

Brandt's treatment of the wrought-iron framework on the side supports is a skilful adaptation of the floral motifs from contemporary textile designs. He captures the technological mood of the machine age with the overlapping roundels, which resemble gear wheels.

MP167 'Méridienne Galbée'

Date: **1923**

Designer: **Pierre Chareau (1883–1950)**

As the name méridienne suggests, a nap on this elegant piece of furniture is most appealing. Madame Helen Bernheim, for whom the bed was made, must have loved reclining in the exotic ambience of her salon, decorated with coromandel wood and bamboo as a backdrop to her collection of Chinese lacquered panels.

With a flared panelled head and rectangular angled foot, the day bed is constructed in palisander with a curved frame (galbée). It is raised on five supports for maximum stability, and each one tapers to a square section and is visibly lifted by the addition of ivory sabots. The original upholstery was in apricot silk velvet to match the Chinese panels.

French architect and designer Pierre Chareau's perfectionism, wit and insistence on quality are all combined in this piece, which was created for a branch of the same family that commissioned his major achievement, 'La Maison de Verre'.

Desk and Chair

Date: *c* 1925

Designers: **Louis Süe (1875–1968) and**

André Mare (1887–1932)

Louis Süe and André Mare established their partnership with the Compaignie des Arts Français in 1919; it continued until 1928. In status and size they were second only to Jacques-Emile Ruhlmann. Süe, a French architect and designer, was responsible for the shape and form of the pieces, while Mare, a painter, supplied the decoration. The pair characterized their work as being for people, not robots. With the increasing demands of the world, they felt that the home should be a place of comfort, harmony and peace.

Often their work was based on eighteenth-century forms, which they simplified and styled in a modern way. For example, this mahogany and leather desk and chair have squared-scroll feet – a distinctive feature of their work at this time. The carved drape effect, the bowed and tapered legs, and the low back of the chair which culminates in a more pronounced scroll, also contribute to the pieces' elegance and refinement.

Desk

Date: **1924**

Designer: **Sir Edward Maufe (1883–1974)**

Made by: **W Rowcliffe**

This is quite early and exotic for English Art Deco and is not typical of work available at the time. The desk was exhibited at the Paris Exposition of 1925 and was one of very few pieces comparable to French designs.

Sir Edward Maufe was an English architect best known for designing Guildford Cathedral. He also made furniture while his wife, Prudence Maufe, worked for Heal & Sons as director of the Mansard Gallery – a showroom for new designs.

The superstructure of the mahogany desk is of stepped form with multiple cupboards made distinctive by the reeded columns. The base has a rectangular top with a frieze drawer and two banks of graduated drawers on either side. The drawers are raised on ebony bun feet and united by a curved foot support and stretcher. The tasselled pulls add a softer element to the severe form, but it is the white-gold finish that attracts the eye.

Console Table

Frenchman Albert Cheuret described himself as a sculptor and designer, and this bronze and marble console table with mirror illustrates the combination of these two skills. It was purchased from the 1925 Paris Exposition by industrialist and politician Rudolphe Tourville as a present for his son, who had successfully qualified as an architect.

The success of this piece rests on its sense of form and proportion. The visually light trapezoid-shaped mirror and pediment is supported on the heavier-looking base. The angle of the owl's wings and the marble and bronze pilaster reflect the mirror's shape, but in a more compressed form, thus maintaining the balance. The table has a sense of quiet authority, engendered as much by its own formality as by the inclusion of the owl with its reputation for wisdom.

Date: **1925**

Designer: **Albert Cheuret (dates unknown)**

Ebony Chair

Date: **c 1925**

Designer: **Clément Rousseau (1872–1950)**

Having initially trained as a sculptor, Clément Rousseau came late to furniture design, but when he did he produced pieces of the highest calibre and quality.

This chair is made of ebony, a very expensive wood and normally used for decoration rather than structure. The fact that this chair has been constructed entirely in ebony speaks for itself.

In form the chair is simple and refined, having a rolled-over top rail, gently bowed apron around the drop-in seat and tapered legs with ivory shoes. Rousseau is less restrained in his use of galuchat (or shagreen, see p. 131) and ivory inlay. The bold sun-burst design, one of the designer's favourite motifs, is used dramatically, with sections of stained galuchat separated by bands of ivory. The galuchat and ivory combination is used on the other elements of the chair and contrasts with the darkness of the wood.

Coquille d'Oeuf Table

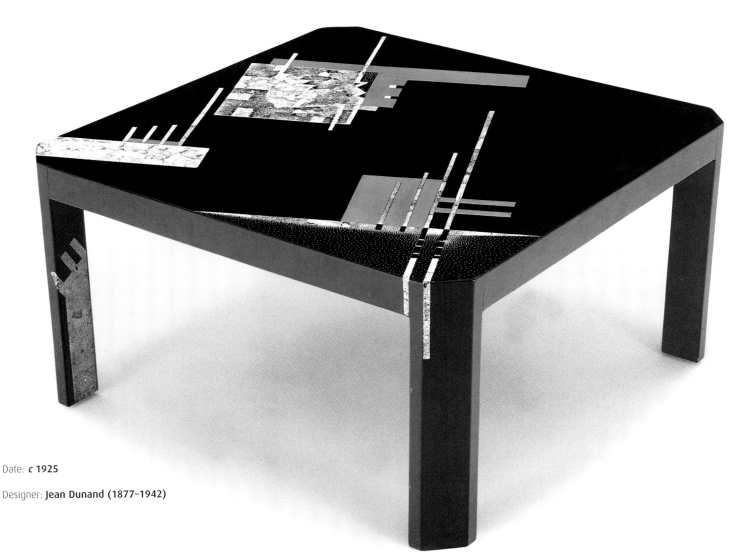

Date: **c 1925**

Designer: **Jean Dunand (1877–1942)**

The geometric pattern, textured effect and quality of the lacquer work on this table result in a most distinctive piece. In its natural state, lacquer (which is obtained from certain trees and harvested in much the same way as rubber is tapped) is an amber-coloured substance, similar to liquid honey. Colours are made by adding vegetable dyes, and although white is not possible, substances such as eggshells can be added to give an impression of white as well as create an interesting texture. The eggshell was separated according to size and individually arranged like a mosaic.

Jean Dunand was revered as a master of his craft and only used traditional lacquer methods. The lacquer process required at least 22 stages to complete, including rubbing, polishing and drying of the many layers, and adding various substances throughout the process. It was not a procedure for the impatient. By 1930 artificial varnishes were being made to create the look of lacquer – in a fraction of the time. There is no comparison in terms of quality between the two but, from a commercial point of view, it brought the lacquered effect to a much wider audience.

Double Bed

Date: *c* 1925

Designer: **Jacques Adnet (1900–84)**

Jacques Adnet was a French designer with a strong Modernist streak. He liked to use exotic materials such as galuchat (or shagreen) to complement more traditional ones like wood, metal and glass. Galuchat is made from the skin of a small spotted dogfish, which is cut into sections and bleached in chlorine. It looks like tightly-packed circles and can be stained in a variety of colours – most often pale green or pink.

The simple form of this bed is raised to exotic heights by the richly covered sections of galuchat.

The headboard is fitted with cupboards on the side and back, while a black-lacquered edge adds definition to the frame. The design enables the bed to be used as a room divider: it would make a stunning addition to a studio apartment.

Jewellery Cabinet On-Stand

This cabinet stands at about 1.4 m (4½ ft) high and just under 50 cm (20 in) wide, and has an inset marble top. The sides and interior of the doors show strongly figured Macassar ebony veneer, and the exterior of the doors and front of the drawers inside are faced with coloured, gilded and tooled leather.

The colour scheme of the leather on the outside of the doors complements the tones of the wood, while the colours on the inside – turquoise, aquamarine, emerald and gold – are more appropriate to jewellery. The stand is elegant and refined, with ribbed, arched tops to the tapered supports which end with carved and stained ivory sabots. The marble top adds weight and stability to the light form.

The piece was made by French painter and designer Clément Mère, for his friends Marcel and Clairette Wolfers. Marcel was a sculptor and son of the famous Belgian Art Nouveau jeweller and silversmith Philippe Wolfers. Mère worked for him occasionally and actually produced some variations of this cabinet for jewellery and cutlery sold by Philippe Wolfers.

Date: *c 1925*

Designer: **Clément Mère (b. 1870, date of death unknown)**

Low Table

Date: *c* 1925

Designer: **Armand-Albert Ratteau (1882–1938)**

This table with its animal imagery and use of bronze is so distinctive, it could only be by French designer Armand-Albert Ratteau. The black marble table top with a white border, which is sunk into the bronze mounts rather than flush with the top, is supported on the backs of stylized pheasants. The birds' legs terminate with the claws clutching a ball – their long arched tails seemingly acting as a counterbalance to support the weight of the top. The birds are cast and decorated with stylized plumage, flowers and shells, and the whole piece is finished with a green patina, known as *verde antico* and very popular with Ratteau.

Ratteau had a very impressive client list. He made this piece for the Duke de Noailles' family, and another version of it was included in his decorative scheme for the Paris couturier Jeanne Lanvin. He sometimes used his designs more than once, but limited them to editions of no more than three.

Skyscraper Chair

Date: **1927**

Designer: **Abel Faidy (1895–1965)**

This chair, by American interior decorator and designer Abel Faidy, owes its form to the stepped outline of Manhattan's skyscrapers. The New York skyline has never failed to impress, although it wasn't as overpowering during the 1920s as it is now. The Chrysler Building (1930) and the Empire State Building (1931) were just a few years away from being built, but the high-rise intent of New York had long been proclaimed.

The maple frame with its raised edge and black recess gives a greater sense of form and dimension. The back extends from the top all the way down to the back foot and shows that the chair is firmly rooted on the ground. The seat and front supports do as little as possible to impede our view of the main feature. Appropriately, a suite of this furniture was made for a penthouse apartment in Chicago.

Fall-Front Secretaire

Date: **1928**

Design Company: **Dominique (1922–70)**

Dominique was a firm of interior decorators founded by Marcel Genevrière and André Domin. The former was an architect, the latter an artist. Their partnership proved very successful and their work was critically acclaimed. They exhibited with a group known as 'Les Cinq', which included Pierre Chareau, Jean Puiforcat, Raymond Templier and Pierre Legrain.

Made in palisander and veneered with sections of galuchat (shagreen) stained in honeyed tones, the secretaire hides its secrets behind closed doors and multiple drawers. The fall-front encloses a fitted interior and the doors beneath open to shelves. It is flanked on either side by its most distinctive feature – a bank of nine small drawers, their size in keeping with the sections of galuchat veneer in the centre. All of these are controlled by the frame of vertical and horizontal lines, and supported on an everted plinth base.

Rosewood Sofa

Date: *c* 1929

Designer: **Marcel Coard (1889–1975)**

At 2.45 m (8 ft) long, this commanding sofa is both comfortable and grand. The plush leather seat cushion, padded back and sides are all tightly controlled by the wooden frame and its double-edged ivory border. One of the most interesting features of the piece – reflecting French designer Marcel Coard's interest in the

Orient – is the frame's outer edge, which has been made of rosewood but carved to simulate rattan. It gives a contrasting texture against the sofa's smooth wood and leather.

The sofa was made for the couturier Jacques Doucet, whose home was like a museum for contemporary arts. This piece sat beneath a huge

painting by Henri Rousseau (*La Charmeuse des Serpents*, now in the Louvre). In the same room there was a Modigliani, a Braque, a carpet by Legrain and a glass door by René Lalique.

Doucet, like a number of couturiers, was a great patron of the French arts, and his collection also included major works by Picasso and Van Gogh.

Cocktail Cabinet

Date: **1929**

Designer: **Ray Hillé (1901–86)**

Made by: **Hillé**

Saloman Hillé started his business in about 1906 as a maker of fine reproduction furniture, providing pieces for Waring & Gillow, Maples and Hamptons, as well as private clients. His daughter Ray joined the firm as a designer in the 1920s, and took over in 1932 when Saloman retired. While maintaining the traditional core of the business, the English designer introduced modern design in the 1920s, and Hillé soon became one of the leading English firms to provide good-quality Art Deco.

The vogue for cocktails, introduced from America, set a new trend in elite circles and the cocktail cabinet was born. This example in satin birch is of shaped rectangular form, over mirrored cupboards on a scroll plinth base. The bowed doors and the central hooped handles break up the surface area of the wood, and the honeyed tones are contrasted with the reflective surface of the mirrors. The interior is partly mirrored and fitted with shelves, drawers and a pull-out shelf to accommodate all the necessary accoutrements for making cocktails.

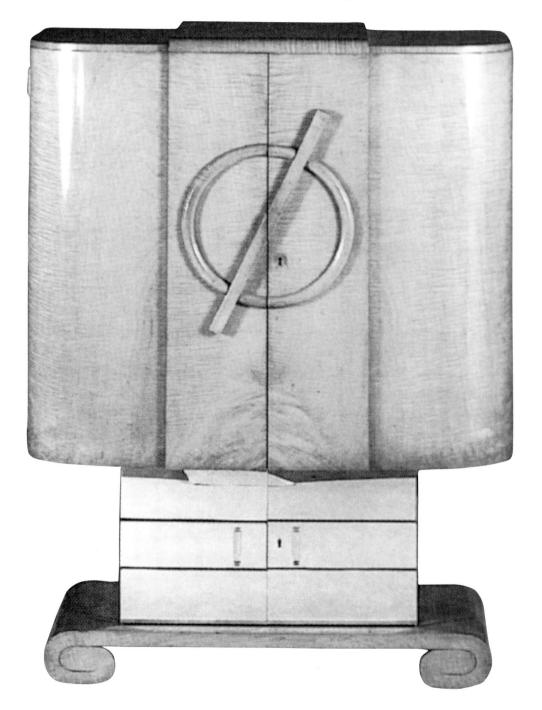

Armchair and Ottoman

Date: *c* 1929

Designer: **Walter von Nessen (1889–1942)**

Not surprisingly, this designer was a pupil of the Bauhaus before emigrating to America. He and his wife Greta formed the Nessen Studio, providing good design for industry, especially in the field of lamps and lighting. It is worth noting the influence of a number of European-trained designers who also emigrated to American during this period, including Kim Weber, Raymond Loewy, Eliel Saarinen, Paul T Frankl and Joseph Urban.

This veneered birch armchair and ottoman were designed for a Hollywood film executive in 1929. Mr and Mrs Glendon Allvine commissioned it for their Modernist East Coast home on Long Island.

The form of the chair is very simple. The back and sides have been made as a single unit, with a seat and arched apron added. There is no ornamentation other than the emphasis given to the chair's outline by the silver leaf and the bud-like feet. Similarly, the stool is plain, its form relying on the relationship of two convex and two concave sides united by the vertical bands of silver leaf.

Three-Fold Screen

Date: **1929**

Designer: **Donald Deskey (1894–1989)**

This screen was designed for the dining room of Mr and Mrs Glendon Allvine's Modernist house on Long Island in America.

Having travelled extensively in Europe, American designer Donald Deskey was familiar with current trends and developments. He had been impressed by the De Stijl group and would have been familiar with Piet Mondrian's paintings, and it is to them that this screen appears to be indebted.

Unusually, each of the canvas-covered folds is a different-sized rectangle, which results in a stepped outline. All have been painted with large, flat, geometric shapes, with strong angles in contrasting silver and black and specifically placed parallel lines in red.

In effect, this is a painting masquerading as a piece of furniture, whose emphasis can be altered by changing the angle of the folds.

Stool

Date: **c 1929**

Designer: **Jules Leleu (1883–1961)**

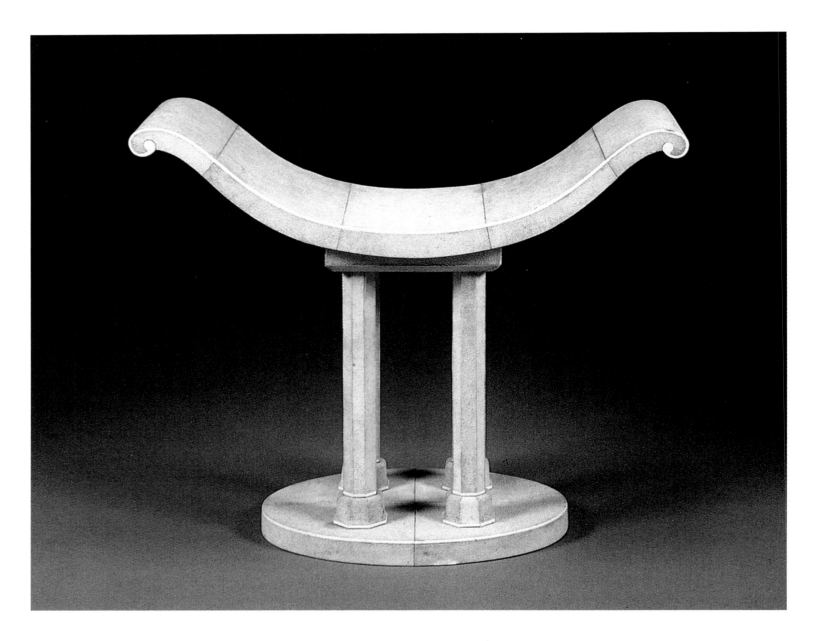

There were many exotic influences on Art Deco, and in France one of these was African art – probably due to their colonial past. One need only think of singer Josephine Baker, who epitomized the spirit of the time, to see how important these influences were.

This stool, by French sculptor and designer Jules Leleu, has a distinctive dished seat, supports and base, and would appear to be based on a headrest made in Africa. The seat is of gentle curved form and covered with segments of galuchat (shagreen). It is finely edged with ivory, which terminates at the end with a scroll. Having a support frame beneath, it is raised on four octagonal columns with shaped ends and an oval base. Again, each of these elements is edged with a fine band of ivory, adding subtle definition to the form.

Dining Table and Chairs

Date: **1929**

Designer: **Eliel Saarinen (1873–1951)**

Eliel Saarinen gained his reputation in Finland as a leading exponent of their Romantic Nationalist style (basically, the Finnish version of Arts and Crafts combined with a little Jugendstil). As with so many other designers at this time, Saarinen's style developed towards cleaner lines and simpler forms to what has been called 'stripped classical Modernism'. He and his wife Loja – a textile designer of some repute – and their son Eero emigrated to America in 1923.

This fir wood dining-room suite was designed for Saarinen's home within the Cranbrook Educational Community, where he was the main architect. Within this community there was an Academy of Arts which Saarinen, as its president, helped to become one of the leading Arts and Design colleges in America. The design for the chairs is particularly refined, with lines on the front and raised ribs on the back. The black detail is picked up on the top and bottom of the chairs' aprons and their tapered legs. The vertical black lines create tapered shapes which are repeated on the segmented table top, thus binding the chairs to the table with a subtle visual link.

Dining Table and Chairs

Date: *c* 1930

Designer: **Anonymous**

Made by: **Epstein, England**

The best English Art Deco furniture tended to be made in the blond woods such as bird's-eye maple and sycamore. Walnut was also popular – either bleached or burred – but was used as much for mediocre pieces as for good ones.

This suite illustrates perfectly two popular features of English Art Deco, namely the curved, U-shaped supports and the veneered tub-back chair. The rectangular table top has rounded corners and a deep apron raised on two broad U-shaped supports, which unite on a plinth base. As a result, the visual weight of the table is reduced, leaving an elegant profile.

The tub-backed chairs are comfortably upholstered but the veneered back gives the form a much more defined line, which is further emphasized by the black edge and feet. The whole suite is veneered in fashionable bird's-eye maple, with its tight figuring and delicately pale colour.

Sofa

Date: *c* 1930

Designer: **Maurice S R Adams (dates unknown)**

By all accounts Maurice Adams was a flamboyant character, and not one to play his talents down. Apparently, he likened himself to the eighteenth-century Adam brothers, Robert and James, and declared that he had created a George V style.

What strikes one first is the use of dramatic contrasts in this piece, such as the blond ripple of the satinwood against the dark watered-silk upholstery. The sofa is approximately 1.8 m (6 ft) long, with stepped sides. The horizontal bands that form the frame are left exposed and hooped around the sofa to connect with the shaped sides at the top of each step. The spaces are filled in with upholstery and the whole is raised on castors to facilitate movement.

The sofa highlights two particular features of Art Deco, one is the stepped profile, the other the use of contrast. In the latter case, it could be mixing colours, materials or textures. Either way, the English architect and designer was aiming for a more dramatic style, based on line and form.

Cloud Suite

Date: *c* 1930

Designer: **Anonymous**

The 'cloud' back suite is one of England's popular contributions to Art Deco design. Formed as a variation on the tub-chair, the back is veneered from the top edge to the bottom, giving the suite a strong but sleek appearance. The decorative figuring of the walnut is also used as intrinsic ornamentation, but it is the billowing shape of the back and the sides, clearly defined in wood, that is so distinctive.

The suite is upholstered in cream leather, which contrasts well with the walnut. At the time cheaper versions were available, including one which had the veneered back but which was upholstered in imitation leather, and another which was the same shape as the original but entirely upholstered. The first variation resulted in poorer quality that can be remedied by reupholstering it in leather, and the second from a loss of definition provided by the clean line of the wood.

Wood Tabouret

Date: *c* 1922

Designer: **Pierre Legrain (1889–1929)**

One could be forgiven for mistaking this unusual tabouret for a tribal artefact. In fact, it was designed by Pierre Legrain, a French designer of book-bindings, and reveals his understanding and knowledge of African art and Cubism.

The avant-garde were fascinated by African art and began forming collections. It was for such a collector, the couturier Jacques Doucet, that Legrain created his most African-inspired pieces. Initially employed to design bindings for Doucet's celebrated book collection, he also made furniture that would complement the couturier's other pieces – including contemporary art, elements of which Legrain often wove into his designs.

It would appear that this stool has been carved from a single block of wood, with the seat and back rest formed as a continuous rectangular curve with canted edges. The rich wood with distinctive figuring is highly polished and contrasts wonderfully with the stacked pyramidal motifs, intaglio-carved and punctuated with gilding. The stool is supported on tapering legs with faceted horn feet, arranged so that the piece slopes forward, adding dynamism.

Console Table

Date: *c* 1930

Designer: **Attributed to William van Alen**

(1883–1954)

This is an interesting example of American Art Deco. The use of metal as a medium for furniture is clearly shown but, unlike in France where wrought iron was favoured, a fine-grade steel has been used. Steel is iron combined with carbon and is one of the strongest metals available; its use made the building of skyscrapers possible.

The Chrysler Building, for which this table was thought to have been made, was designed by American architect William van Alen and has a distinctive stainless-steel top. Along with the Empire State Building, it is one of the most popular Art Deco buildings in the world.

The table works well because it is bold but not too elaborate. The shaped, polished black-marble top sits within its metal frame on six scrolled supports separated by five shorter stems on a stepped marble base. The spaces created in this design are as important as the solids, and therefore the colour of the wall behind would have been considered in the table's placement.

Sideboard

Date: **1931**

Designer: **Michel Dufet (1888–1985)**

The weight of unusual-looking sideboard is supported centrally instead of at each corner. As a result, a backboard has been attached at the bottom so that it can be secured to the wall (a necessary compromise for the look, although perhaps not everyone's idea of convenience).

The early decorative style of French furniture designer and decorator Michel Dufet had developed into a more Modernist approach by the 1930s. This sideboard falls into the latter phase, having a stepped edge to the top and rounded front corners. The two doors, enclosing shelves, flank the four vertical supports faced in duralumin (an alloy of aluminium, copper and other metals), and the bottom edge is rounded. It has a sleek appearance, with the vertical grain of the palisander and duralumin bands counterbalancing the dominant horizontal form.

In 1927 Dufet joined the art studio of retailer Le Bûcheron. He felt that there were a limited number of people who could afford exclusive pieces and, in keeping with the spirit of the new century, that it was better to offer good design to, say, 20 or 30 people at a more reasonable price, than wait for one rich patron.

Knee-Hole Desk (M-315-W)

Date: **1931**

Designer: **Count Alexis de Sakhnoffsky (1901–64)**

Made by: **Heywood-Wakefield, USA**

Count Alexis de Sakhnoffsky established his name as a designer in the automobile industry, and his work on custom-made cars for Studebaker, Cord and Auburn is evident in the streamlined design of this desk. It also shows how technology, particularly in the field of aerodynamics, had an impact on domestic design.

All the edges of this solid birch desk are rounded, with the exception of the bottom edge of the frieze drawer which seems to cut through the air to join the two pedestals. The two banks of drawers, with their distinctive in-curved fronts, have drawer handles reminiscent of aeroplane wings – very much in

keeping with Norman Bel Geddes's belief that the tear drop was the perfect streamlined shape. All the drawers are flush with one another or, in the case of the frieze drawer, flush with the top edge, and this uncluttered structure adds to the American designer's quest for streamlined simplicity.

Elbow Chair

Date: **1934**

Designer: **Russel Wright (1904–76)**

Made by: **Attributed to Heywood-Wakefield, USA**

Russel Wright was one of America's most influential designers. He advocated a more informal approach to domestic living and designed a wide variety of pieces to serve this philosophy, including a sofa in moveable sections and upholstered furniture that was coordinated rather than matching. He even wrote a book, with his wife Mary, called *A Guide to Easier Living* (1951). In America Wright is a household name, thanks to a set of tableware he designed in 1937 called American Modern.

Like a number of Americans, Wright was searching for his own Modernist style, rather than slavishly copying the tubular-steel designers in Europe. This chair is a reaction to that sterile geometry and to designers more interested in the 'look' of a piece, rather than needs of the people using it. The shaped and carved arms are supported on curved and tapering supports, and the chair has a canvas slingback and an calfskin upholstered seat. The use of calfskin could possibly be a reference to cattle ranches – an integral part of American culture.

Eva Armchair

Date: **1934–6**

Designer: **Bruno Mathsson (1907–88)**

Reissued by: **Dux, Sweden**

The Eva armchair represents a more humane approach to Modernism, in keeping with Alvar Aalto's psychophysical theories about design. As a cabinet-maker's son, Swedish designer Bruno Mathsson was able to experiment with bentwood and laminates for his research into the support structure needed to produce the perfect chair for the human anatomy.

As a result, he designed different chairs to meet different lifestyle requirements, including working, sitting and reclining. He also favoured a webbed seat and back in either hemp or leather, which he felt offered the most support.

The chair is made in two sections – the solid birch frame for the back and seat, upholstered in hemp webbing, and the arms and legs. The accentuated curve of the arm and the back are the most pronounced organic features. Like this chair, most of Mathsson's earlier designs were made in his father's workshops and sold directly to the customer.

Serving Table

Date: *c* 1935

Designer: **Gio Ponti (1891–1979)**

This rosewood serving table forms part of an elegant dining-room suite and is visually restful as well as stylish. The table top has a raised edge and the apron below has three flush-fitting drawers, all covered in parchment. It is raised on two waisted, fluted supports, which are united at the top and bottom by stretchers, both of which are carved with zigzag banding that joins the fluting on the columns. The whole piece is elevated on a rouge marble plinth.

The two design features that make this piece exceptional are the waisted uprights and the undulating line of the stretcher directly beneath the table top. The latter works beautifully against the straight white line of the apron and drawers.

As an architect, designer, teacher, writer and magazine editor (*Domus and Stile*), Gio Ponti had a huge influence on Italian design. Personally, he tried to combine his country's classical heritage with the influence of the Italian Futurists to create a modern new style.

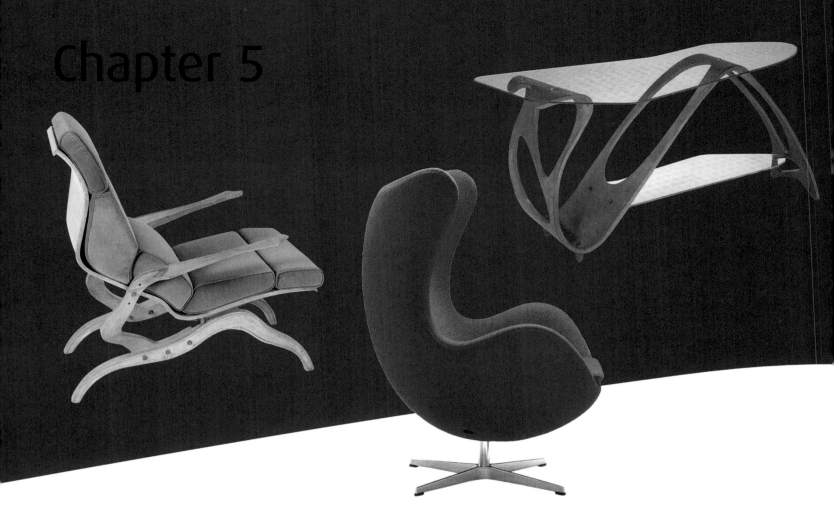

Chapter 5

Mid-Century Modern

The Second World War brought changes to people's lives the world over. Many European designers left their homelands because of their religion or because they knew their creativity would be restricted. Some, like Friederich Adler, died in Auschwitz.

For most countries at war with Nazism, there was rationing of everything. Albert Speer, Hitler's architect, noted that the democratic countries opposing Hitler suffered more than the Germans under dictatorship. Hitler realized the need to keep his people happy, and ensured that consumer goods were readily available.

In Britain, as early as July 1940, timber and tubular steel were banned for the manufacture of furniture, and in 1942 The

Advisory Committee on Utility Furniture was born. It produced furniture that was sparing on raw materials but which was well designed, manufactured and priced. It was available to people who had been bombed out of their homes, or to newlyweds.

In 1942 America restricted the use of raw materials, and the furniture industry used fibre boards instead of natural woods. Some of their best designers – Raymond Loewy, Walter Dorwin Teague and Norman Bel Geddes – were drafted in to help with design briefs, such as plans for a mobile field hospital.

After the war many countries suffered from lack of funding, scarcity of raw materials, labour shortages and unsuitable production

facilities. Governments established bodies to encourage new designs, and held exhibitions such as the Britain Can Make It in 1946, and The Festival of Britain in 1951.

The 1950s heralded a new era in design, with inspiration coming from Italy, Scandinavia and America. The period favoured light, spacious interiors and vivid colours to counteract the drab war years. The plain functionalism of the Modernists prevailed, but with a more organic approach. Motifs reflecting the age, such as molecular patterns and space-age imagery, were popular.

Scandinavian designers showed a sympathy to natural materials. They took full advantage of machine production and used bold shapes and curves. Another approach, best characterized by Gio Ponti in Italy, favoured handcraft and more traditional means of decoration, without losing sight of current events. In contrast to this, designers such as Charles Eames and Eero Saarinen included production methods as part of the design and creative process.

New materials became available (largely through technology developed during the war), offering a wealth of possibilities to designers. Du Pont in New York had created nylon in 1939, and a new lightweight plastic called polyethylene was first used commercially by the Tupper Corporation.

Aircraft technology had developed lighter, stronger plywood, and the merits of fibreglass and glass-reinforced plastic – used in protective domes for aircraft radar – were undisputed. In Italy Marco Zanuso worked with the Pirelli company on the development of foam rubber, which transformed the shape of upholstery.

The best design of the period was characterized by a unity of form and function, that was good-looking and practical. However, the period also produced its fair share of kitsch artefacts and design horrors, but these have not been included here!

BA Chair

Date: **1945**

Designer: **Ernest Race (1913–64)**

Made by: **Race Furniture Ltd**

Ernest Race was one of England's leading post-war furniture designers. Here, he shows great ingenuity in the production of a chair made in aluminium taken from scrapped war planes.

Even though the war had finished by the time this chair was shown, the Advisory Committee on Utility Furniture allowed Race to make it, so long as he didn't use solid wood as rationing was still in place. It was first shown at the Britain Can Make It exhibition in 1946, and continued in production until the late 1960s.

The cast-aluminium frame is stove-enamelled and is of tapering V-section with a plywood seat, back and rests upholstered for comfort. The chair is very light because of the aluminium, and there are versions with or without arms. He went on to add a sideboard and table in the same series, still using the aluminium, but with the doors, sides and tops veneered with mahogany. The BA chair won a gold medal in 1951 at the Milan IX Triennale

Screen and Pair of Lounge Chairs

Date: **1946**

Designers: **Charles Eames (1907–78) and**

Ray Eames (1912–88)

Made by: **Herman Miller Furniture Company**

American designers Charles and Ray Eames's involvement with plywood began in earnest when Charles co-designed a chair with Eero Saarinen for the Organic Design in Home Furnishings Competition in 1940. When Charles and Ray moved to California in 1941, they made splints and stretchers in plywood for the US Navy. This led to further experiments with the technical possibilities of plywood. Hitherto, the most successful designs in this medium had been in Europe.

The Folding Screen in Wood (FSW) is made in six moulded sections of plywood with a walnut-veneered finish. It is united by a full-length canvas 'hinge'. Each of the six folds is from an identical mould, allowing easy and economic production, and the canvas hinge allows flexible display and easy storage and packaging when folded. It is a wonderfully fluid example of organic Modernism.

The lounge chairs in calico ash plywood (LCWs) are made of five elements cut from a single sheet of ply, moulded and bent. Each element remains separate but is united to form the whole. The seat and back are moulded and set at an angle to follow the contours of the body. They are joined to the tapering supports by shock-mounts made of black rubber. These absorbers add another degree of flexibility to the natural spring of the central support.

Womb Chair

Date: **1946**

Designer: **Eero Saarinen (1910–61)**

Made by: **Knoll**

The organic Modernism of Finnish architect and designer Eero Saarinen is well illustrated in his Womb chair. Apparently, he tried to think of a different name in case people were offended, but nothing else worked as well.

The chair was loosely based on one Saarinen had co-designed with Charles Eames for a competition on Organic Design in Home Furnishings, held at the Museum of Modern Art in New York in 1940. The Womb chair was broader and bigger than the competition one, however, and Saarinen's later effort was a bid to produce a twentieth-century version of the traditional Victorian armchair. He was aiming for a less conservative form that would be appropriate for a more casual lifestyle.

The chair is made from plastic reinforced with fibreglass; it is upholstered and raised on chromium-plated steel supports and was produced by Knoll, one of the most progressive furniture makers of the second half of the twentieth century. Saarinen envisioned an enveloping chair which would enable the sitter to draw up his legs while also supporting his back, arms and shoulders.

Peacock Armchair

Date: **1947**

Designer: **Hans J Wegner (b. 1914)**

Made by: **Johannes Hansen, Denmark**

Much Modernist furniture designed in post-war Scandinavia utilized natural materials, and this is exemplified by Danish designer and architect, Hans J Wegner.

The Peacock armchair was a new interpretation of a traditional Windsor chair. However, here the broad ash wood hooped-back is more pronounced and generous. Enclosed within the hoop are radiating, flattened spindles extending across the back in a curve, reminiscent of peacock feathers. These offer support for the sitter's back, and are more comfortable than the round spindles of the Windsor chair. The teak arms slope backwards for comfort, their supports extending through the paper cord seat, linking to a stretcher for added stability.

In 1947 production and design processes ran simultaneously, and the prototype Peacock chair was sold (by mistake) before the final construction drawings were completed. Production was put back a year, but the design has proved popular to this day.

'Listen To Me' Couch

Date: **1947**

Designer: **Edward J Wormley (1907–95)**

Made by: **Dunbar Furniture**

This piece of furniture by American designer and interior decorator, Edward J Wormley, is simple and spare, its title a reference to the psychiatrist's couch. The psychoanalyst and the couch are very much a part of the twentieth century and have been brought into popular culture. They are synonymous with unburdening and relaxing.

The gentle undulating frame, made of laminated white maple and cherry wood, is raised on tapering angled supports united by metal rods and an X-shaped tension cable. The whole piece appears light and unpretentious, its character quiet and undemanding. The comfortable, upholstered surface sits lightly on the seemingly delicate frame, giving the couch a hammock-like quality, only with legs.

Chieftain Armchair

Date: **1949**

Designer: **Finn Juhl (1912–89)**

Made by: **Niels Vodder, Denmark**

The structural elements of this walnut and leather chair comprise verticals that are turned and tapered, and horizontals that are flat and shaped. The angled supports for the sides are also curved, and all the elements are left exposed and arranged at various angles. Each element has a purpose, but the number makes the chair appear complex. The calming features include the curved back, seat and armrests whose soft shape have a time-worn appearance.

Finn Juhl, a Danish architect and designer, was one of the leading exponents of what became known as 'Danish Modern'. The chair is made by Niels Vodder, and was typical of the quality one had come to expect from the master craftsman.

The chair is reputed to have been named after King Frederich IX sat on it at the opening of an exhibition. A journalist suggested that it should now be called the King's chair, but Juhl considered this a little on the excessive side, and suggested the name Chieftain instead.

Antony Chair

Date: **1950**

Designer: **Jean Prouvé (1901–84)**

The furniture designs of Jean Prouvé are strongly indicative of his engineering background. He 'industrialized' pieces using tubular metal and steel and zinc sheets often constructed from prefabricated components. In the 1920s the French designer had already begun to make prefabricated desks, with interchangeable compartments, for the Parisian Electricity Company.

This chair was originally designed for the University of Strasbourg. It was manufactured by Prouvé's own company, which he founded in 1931. (He gave up furniture design when he left the company in 1953.)

Prouvé preferred to leave the techniques of construction – such as welding marks and unfinished surfaces – in evidence. The treatment of the metal on this chair and black paintwork juxtaposes with the smooth surface and warm colour of the wooden seat, which flares gently at the beginning and end of the generous curve. The harmony expressed is very much in keeping with the principles of Yin and Yang.

'Arabesco' Plywood and Glass Tea Table

Date: *c* 1950

Designer: **Carlo Mollino (1905–73)**

Made by: **Apelli, Varesio & Co., Italy**

Much of Italian architect and designer Carlo Mollino's furniture was designed to complement the curves of the human body. The organic forms of his chairs, desks and tables are reminiscent of the twisted branches of trees or deer's antlers, and he described himself as 'a streamlined surrealist'. This extraordinary table is one of his most imaginative biomorphic designs.

Aerodynamic streamlining, moulded plywood technology used in aeroplane manufacture and his interest in flying and aerobatics were influential in forming Mollino's idiosyncratic style. The possible influence of Jean Arp's wooden reliefs and Henry Moore's sculptures is also evident here.

The maple plywood table resembles a primordial creature. Its fluid undulating curves and asymmetric apertures demand our concentration on all sides. The tension, like a spring desperate to unwind, is held in check by the two horizontal glass sheets fixed with brass fasteners. The table top's shape was apparently taken from a drawing of a woman's torso by Leonor Fini. Mollino's personal statement adequately sums up his thoughts: 'The best explanation of one's work is contained in its silent ostentation.'

Armchair

Date: *c* 1950

Designer: **Carlo Graffi (dates unknown)**

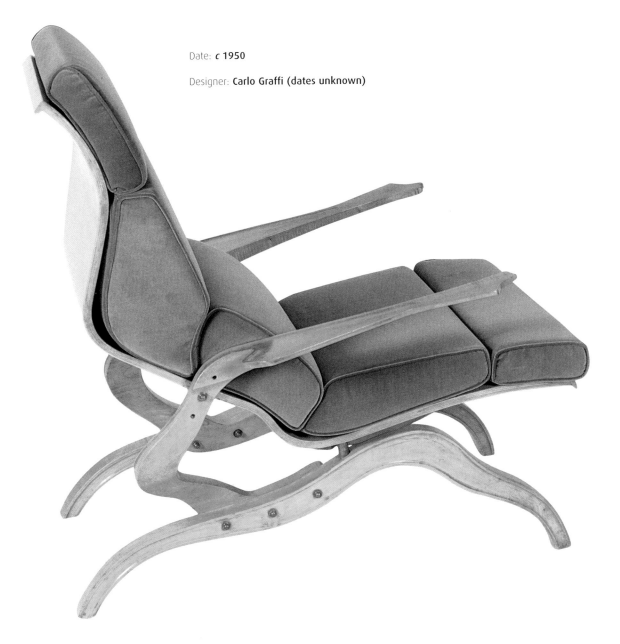

It is hard to imagine a chair more organic than this one unless we return to the work of Antonio Gaudí. The whole piece looks as though it has evolved under natural pressures around the body of the sitter, rather than been designed to a rigid formula. The segmented cushions are reminiscent of the body of an insect and have been designed to support and fit the contours of the body.

The back and seat of the chair, which is made of birch and birch laminate, are moulded from a single sheet of plywood in an undulating line, which gives an unlikely profile. The cushions make this possible because they fill in the unnatural spaces and take the appropriate form for the human body. The screws that join the legs, armrests and body together are deliberately left exposed.

Italian architect and designer Carlo Graffi was a contemporary of Carlo Mollino's. Like him, he belongs to the organic school of 1950s design, favouring Expressionism and fantasy, rather than the sterile rationalism inherited from the Modernists.

Lady Armchair

Date: **1951**

Designer: **Marco Zanuso (b. 1916)**

Made by: **Arflex, Milan**

The materials, their properties and the production methods needed to harness them were always a major part of the creative process for Italian designer Marco Zanuso. Only when these were in hand could he consider the aesthetics of a piece.

Although foam rubber had been available since the 1930s, its potential was not realized until the beginning of the 1950s. Pirelli had begun to explore the possibilities of using it in cars and brought Zanuso in to explore its potential in mass-produced furniture, who swiftly realized how dramatically it would alter the nature and form of upholstery.

The first pieces to take advantage of Zanuso's research were chairs and sofas made in 1951 and shown at the IX Triennale in Milan. The Lady armchair was among them and received a gold medal. To allow for mass production, each of the four elements (back, seat and two sides) were upholstered separately. Depending on the level of support required, foam of varying density and firmness was used over the wooden (later metal) frame, and covered with fabric. Only then was the chair assembled as the finished article.

'Architettura' Bureau/Cabinet

Date: **1951**

Designers: **Gio Ponti (1891–1979)**

and Piero Fornasetti (1913–88)

Gio Ponti was a highly regarded architect, a prolific writer and one of Italy's principal twentieth-century designers. He was a strong supporter of Italian craft, recognizing the important link between the workshop and mass production. He promoted modern design in the influential journals *Domus* and *Stile*, which he directed for many years. His chair designs are probably the best known, particularly the remarkably light Superleggera (1955), which became a huge international success after being put into production by Cassina in 1957. Ponti formed a collaboration with Piero Fornasetti after meeting him in the late 1930s, and became one of his staunchest supporters.

Resembling a giant doll's house, this magnificent bureau/cabinet is a masterful amalgam of two great talents. The upper part draws the viewer into the trompe l'oeil architectural interior, where a central metal alcove is flanked by three glass shelves. In the middle section, a fall-front bureau depicts a row of three arches within, and below this, three long drawers depict yet another architectural interior – the whole decorated in monochrome and raised on four tapering legs. Fornasetti had a particular interest in the works of the Victorian architect William Burges, and his influence can be seen here.

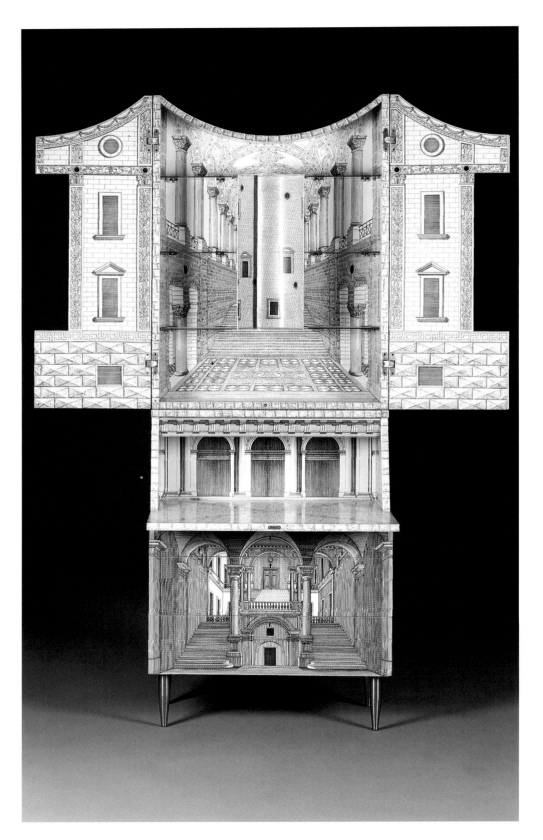

DKR-2 Chair

Date: **1951**

Designers: **Charles Eames (1907–78)**

and Ray Eames (1912–88)

Made by: **Herman Miller, USA**

The Herman Miller Furniture Company rose like a phoenix from the old Star Furniture Company in 1923, when Herman Miller and Dirk Jan De Pree bought half the company. It wasn't until 1930, when Gilbert Rohde was appointed head of design, that the company became involved with Modernism, and established itself as one of America's leading producers of contemporary furniture.

Gilbert Rohde died in 1944 but his legacy was continued by George Nelson, the company's design consultant. In addition to designing pieces for them, he also collaborated with other creative forces including American architect and designer, Charles Eames.

A list of designers' work produced by Herman Miller reads like a who's who of modern design, and includes Isamu Noguchi, Poul Kjaerholm and Verner Panton to name but a few. The company is still going strong.

Armchair

Date: **1952**

Designer: **Frank Lloyd Wright (1867–1959)**

Made by: **Domore Chair Company of Elkhart, Indiana for the Price Company Tower, Bartlesville, Oklahoma**

An extraordinary chair by Frank Lloyd Wright, arguably America's greatest architect and designer. Although he is best known for his Prairie-style architecture and his Arts and Crafts interiors, Lloyd Wright was a very modern designer. He embraced the machine and its potential, and even in his early work his designs were plain and rectilinear.

This chair is an exercise in geometry, its form based around the hexagon. The upholstered seat and back have equal sides, but the base does not. The drama of the seat is played out with a rounded exposed underbelly caught within the four aluminium arms and hexagonal frame, like a gemstone set within its collet. The other distinctive feature is the use of faceting on all the metal edges and surfaces, making full use of the dynamic effect of light and shadow. From a maintenance and production point of view, the chair is also extremely versatile – with interchangeable parts allowing a secretary's, an executive's and visitor's version.

Walnut Desk

Date: **1952**

Designer: **Franco Cavatorta (b. 1925)**

Made by: **Silvio Cavatorta, Italy**

This desk is divided into three clear elements, the writing surface, the storage system and the supports. These, in turn, create a fourth factor, namely the spaces and shapes evoked. The broad sweep of the curved top is mirrored by the under-tier below, and has soft, rounded edges. The K-shaped supports cut through the second tier to unite the solid elements together; their power and strength support the drawers which are carefully balanced like scales. The drawers are recessed within their frame, and the handles are recessed within the drawers and mirror their shape.

The branch-like supports were a popular design feature of Italian furniture in the 1950s. Here, the front leg has a more pronounced forward thrust like the support above it. Italian architect and designer Franco Cavatorta was fortunate to have a cabinet-maker father, who could lovingly recreate his work.

Diamond Lounge Chair

Date: **1951–2**

Designer: **Arieto (Harry) Bertoia (1915–78)**

Made by: **Knoll**

Whether he was sculpting or designing furniture, Italian-born American designer Harry Bertoia always worked in metal. He combined the inherent qualities of metal with the sculptural principles of space and form, and described his grid-steel chairs as 'Mostly made of air, just like sculpture. Space passes right through them.'

Bertoia won a scholarship to Cranbrook Academy of Art and subsequently became a teacher there. He worked briefly with Charles and Ray Eames before accepting an offer from Florence Knoll, who he had met at Cranbrook. With the freedom Knoll Associates offered him, he was able to concentrate on his sculpture and also design his now famous mesh-steel lounge and side chairs. With the aid of Knoll technicians, the means of mass production was secured. The mesh was effectively moulded into shape and then fixed to the wire metal stands. It could be chromium-plated or painted, with cushions or upholstery added.

Four-Fold Lacquered Screen

Date: *c* 1953

Designer: **Piero Fornasetti (1913–88)**

In Piero Fornasetti's view, no domestic accessory was too humble for a makeover. This four-fold screen would be inconsequential without the Italian decorator and designer's inventive touch. Under his direction the piece is magical and fun – the panels are silk-screen printed in colours against a white background, and give a panoramic view of hot-air balloons floating effortlessly above a rural landscape, some escaping at the top. The screen is raised on eight sturdy castors for easy mobility.

As a student, Fornasetti was frustrated at the lack of classical training available. As a result, he surrounded himself with books on the history of craft, treatises on design and architectural pattern books. He taught himself painting, engraving, printing, and was influenced by the Novecento group of artists and architects.

From his premises in Milan, Fornasetti undertook the manufacturing and marketing of his products, ensuring that the technique of each printed decoration remained secret. His love of drawing and his skilled draughtsmanship formed the basis of his work, and was particularly popular during the 1950s and 1960s. Even then, he could be considered an anomaly of post-war Italian design due to his rejection of Modernism.

Sideboard

Date: **1954**

Designer: **Robert Heritage (b. 1927)**

Made by: **A G Evans, Great Britain**

Britain firmly believed that its socio-economic problems could be solved by promoting itself to the world as modern and innovative, encouraging export orders so valuable in the climate of austerity present just after the war. Maximum exposure would be gained by holding prestigious exhibitions such as Britain Can Make It in 1946. With the huge redevelopment of bomb-blasted cities and towns, and the need to rehouse people in new environments, it was important that furniture and furnishings keep up with the change of lifestyle.

It was in this climate that Robert Heritage designed his screen-printed sideboard, with its solid wood carcass and ebonized top and sides contrasting dramatically against the pale birch veneers. Below the three frieze drawers with recessed handles are two cupboards flanking a central compartment with a drop-down flap, the fronts of which are silk-screen printed with a black linear design, depicting overlapping buildings in flattened perspective reminiscent of Piero Fornasetti's work. The whole is raised on four legs, each formed from three metal rods linked by an inverted conical foot.

P40 Chaise Longue

Date: **1954**

Designer: **Osvaldo Borsani (1911–85)**

Made by: **Tecno SpA**

Tecno was founded by Italian designer Osvaldo Borsani and his brother Fulgenzio as an extension of the family business, which was run by their father Gaetano. The aim of the company was to produce Osvaldo's technically sophisticated furniture, of which this chaise longue is an excellent example. All the main elements of its design are adjustable, enabling a total of 486 positional variables.

The chaise has a core frame of pressed steel and the seat and back are segmented into four parts. It can be moved into an upright position, the metal footrest can be retracted and the leg support folded completely back underneath to form an armchair. However, the chair is at its most elegant and comfortable in the reclined position. The arms can be used as rests or pushed down out of the way – a manoeuvre made possible by the spring-steel bands enclosed within black rubber sleeves. The whole is upholstered with fabric over latex or polyfoam, and supported on steel supports with very small castors at the back.

Steel and Cane Chair

Date: **1955**

Designer: **Poul Kjaerholm (1929–80)**

Made by: **E Kold Christensen, Copenhagen**

This chromium-plated and cane chair is a perfect example of clean, functional Modernism. It comprises only three elements: the seat, the legs and the clamps that unite them. In keeping with Modernist principles, Danish architect and designer Poul Kjaerholm designed for mass production. In the case of chairs and sofas, he tended towards steel or metal for structural elements, and natural materials for coverings or upholstery. (When this chair was first made it was sold with a choice of four leather coverings, or a canvas one; the cane shown here was introduced in 1957.)

Kjaerholm has used spring-steel for the chair's legs and frame, which gives it flexibility and additional comfort. However, spring-steel does not weld particularly well because of the movement, necessitating the need for a clamp system with Allen screws to unite the seat to the legs.

Rocking Stool

Date: *c* 1955

Designer: **Isamu Noguchi (1904–88)**

Made by: **Knoll**

The idea of a rocking stool (right) is certainly a novel one, and matches the informality associated with the stool as a piece of furniture.

The design was a natural for adaptation and varying sized tables were made. The wooden seat is dished, and united to the rocking base by intersecting V-shaped metal supports. There are two stories about the stool's inception. One features Hans Knoll who, having seen a plastic stool in Isamu Noguchi's studio, asked him to design one that incorporated metal rods. The other says the stool was inspired by an African one which belonged to a friend of Noguchi's and irritated him by its lack of movement. As a result, Noguchi's design enables the user to tilt it at any point in its circumference.

Noguchi was a prominent American sculptor. His furniture designs are refined and simple, and show the sculptor's eye for space and form.

Large Marshmallow Sofa

Date: *c* 1955

Designer: **George Nelson Associates**

Made by: **Herman Miller, USA**

There are few pieces of furniture that look good enough to eat, but this is definitely one of them. In addition, it is larger than the normal 18-cushion version, which makes it all the more sumptuous!

Developed by Irving Harper at George Nelson Associates, the idea of attaching individual cushions to an exposed tubular-steel frame was revolutionary. However, because it required a huge amount of handwork, the concept of mass production was not an easy brief to fulfil. Neither did the sofa relate to conventional modern design, and its production life was brief.

The Marshmallow sofa is an extremely practical piece of furniture. The circular latex foam cushions are upholstered in easy-to-clean vinyl, and the removal and replacement of individual cushions would have been easier and less expensive than reupholstering a more conventional sofa.

The colour combination pictured proved the most popular. Arranged in what appears to be a random manner, the Smartie-like cushions have actually been cleverly arranged to discourage the eye from settling on any one spot.

Butterfly Stool

Date: **1956**

Designer: **Sori Yanagi (b. 1915)**

Made by: **Tendo Mokko, Japan**

This stool has a calm and assured elegance. It radiates centuries of Oriental tradition, neatly encapsulated in a New Age material, and is Sori Yanagi's most celebrated work – an icon of modern industrialized Japan.

The piece is fashioned from two identical elements in moulded plywood – positioned as a mirror-image of each other and linked by a metal stretcher. Calligraphic in profile, it resembles a pair of hands touching at the wrists with palms held skywards as though yielding a religious offering. Alternatively, it could be interpreted as symbolizing the release of something, like letting a butterfly go.

Yanagi's father Soetsu Yanagi was the leading advocate of the Mingei Movement, which asserted that true beauty in product design should be found in crafts that are used by everyone; not made with a self-conscious effort to create beauty, but designed to cater to the needs of everyday life. In 1936 Yanagi Snr founded the Japanese Folk Crafts Museum in Tokyo, and Sori was raised in this environment.

Lounge Chair and Ottoman

Date: **1957**

Designers: **Charles Eames (1907–78)**

and Ray Eames (1912–88)

Made by: **Herman Miller, USA**

This chair and ottoman have become a design classic of the twentieth century. Thanks to their aesthetic appeal and comfort, they are still produced today. Until 1990, the plywood used was rosewood, but it was switched to walnut and cherry due to the increasing scarcity of rosewood. Originally they could have been purchased with fabric, leather or naughahyde cushions, but after 1962 it was only available in leather.

The chair is made with three sections of curved plywood upholstered with button-backed cushions. The two back sections are united by cast-aluminium bars, and the seat is supported on a swivel and rocking base with five polished feet. The chair was designed so that it could be assembled by one person with a screwdriver, and the Eames's made an amusing, speeded-up film to illustrate this claim. Not surprisingly, the piece won a gold medal at the XII Milan Triennale in 1960.

Egg Chair and Ottoman

Date: **1957**

Designer: **Arne Jacobsen (1902–71)**

Made by: **Fritz Hansen, Denmark**

The Egg chair was one of Arne Jacobsen's three major seat designs of the 1950s, along with the Ant chair (1952) and the Swan chair (1957). It was produced as part of the furnishings for the Royal Hotel in Copenhagen – a major commission for the Danish architect and designer.

This chair expresses a sense of comfort and stability, as well as making a strong sculptural statement. The shell is formed from moulded fibreglass-reinforced polyurethane. It was upholstered with latex foam, covered with leather, and is supported on a cast-aluminium four-point pedestal base, allowing a

tilting and swivelling action. Although lacking in total originality – the form echoes Eero Saarinen's Womb armchair of 1946 – it has nevertheless been in continuous production since 1957, and should be considered as one of the most influential post-war furniture designs.

Conoid Bench

Date: *c* 1958

Designer: **George Nakashima (1905–90)**

American George Nakashima trained as an architect, but followed a career as a wood craftsman. His personal style shows an amalgam of influences, from vernacular American to Japanese crafts and construction techniques. The decorative effects of knots, burrs and random graining within a cross-section of timber delighted Nakashima, who also used the rough, un-trimmed outside of the tree (called the 'free edge') to great effect.

His work harks back to the Shaker furniture of the eighteenth century, with its emphasis on simple living. His designs were original, but were also produced in limited numbers, thus ensuring a consistently high level of quality and integrity.

This bench looks what it is – a well-made, practical piece of furniture, with just the right amount of finishing to prevent it from looking bland. It has a large irregular section of ash for the seat which is supported on four tapering legs. The back rest is formed by a row of 23 shaped spindles, arranged in a curve and united by an ash top-rail tapering at the ends.

Harp Chair

Date: **1958**

Designer: **Jørgen Høvelskov (dates unknown)**

Made by: **Jørgen Christensen, Denmark**

The title of this chair is misleading. Far from taking his inspiration from a musical instrument, Danish designer Jørgen Høvelskov based the chair's shape on the bow section of a Viking sailing ship, with the central element presumably being indicative of a mast, and the flag line representing the halyards.

The chair is constructed from solid birch with the line woven loom-like between the three curved supports and the upright. The arrangement of the lines tapering towards the top plays with perspectives and creates a dramatic optical effect, recalling the 'Linear Constructions' of the sculptor Naum Gabo a decade earlier.

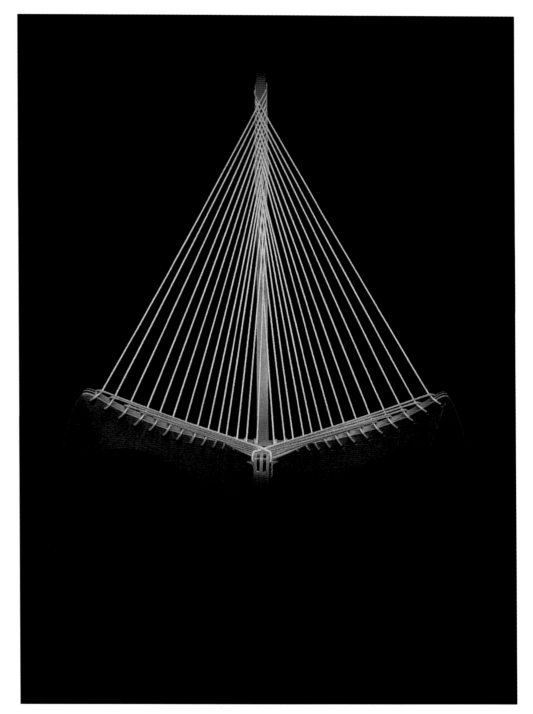

Wood Tables

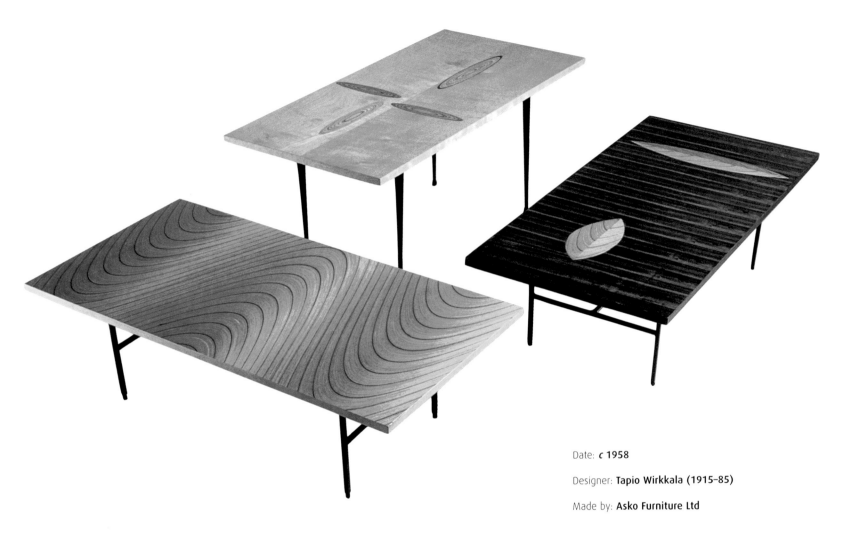

Date: *c* 1958

Designer: **Tapio Wirkkala (1915–85)**

Made by: **Asko Furniture Ltd**

During the second half of the twentieth century Tapio Wirkkala was considered Finland's most versatile and influential designer. He trained as a sculptor before moving into the decorative arts, and favouring naturalistic forms, he wished to create pieces using traditional Finnish materials and techniques. Surprisingly, the aesthetics of these techniques have survived under the patronage of large industrial firms where cutting-edge technology

has been used without the loss of artistic integrity.

Wirkkala worked as a freelance designer for Asko Furniture – a company that aimed to meet the demand for well-made pieces designed with small apartments in mind. These tables are a perfect example, with their rectangular tops raised on tapering metal legs. The linear graining acts as a wonderful foil for the inlaid motifs, fashioned in laminated woods of varying colours to produce banding.

The motifs include leaf-forms (although not direct copies), and cosmic rings influenced by ventures into space, perhaps, such as the launch of the Sputnik satellite in 1957. Whatever the inspiration they have a 'simplicity and eloquence of understatement', much like the leaf-shaped wooden platter to which this quote, taken from an edition of the magazine *House Beautiful* published in 1952, refers.

Cone Chairs

Date: **1958**

Designer: **Verner Panton (1926–98)**

Made by: **Fritz Hansen, Denmark**

Verner Panton worked in the architectural practice of fellow Danish designer Arne Jacobsen, before opening his own design office in Switzerland in 1955.

Panton felt that it was the responsibility of all designers to make full use of the newly available technologies and materials. Over a long period of time, he experimented with the concept of creating a single-piece cantilever chair. He achieved this aim in 1967, producing the first commercial polyester and fibreglass stacking chair through Herman Miller.

Almost a decade earlier, while he was still looking for a new furniture vocabulary, he designed the Cone chair. It was a truly futuristic concept, constructed in shaped sheet metal with latex-foam cushioning and upholstered in woven fabric or vinyl. The chair was supported as if balancing on a cast-aluminium cruciform base and has a nostalgic feel – reminding us of childhood spinning tops or ice-cream cones.

Chapter 6

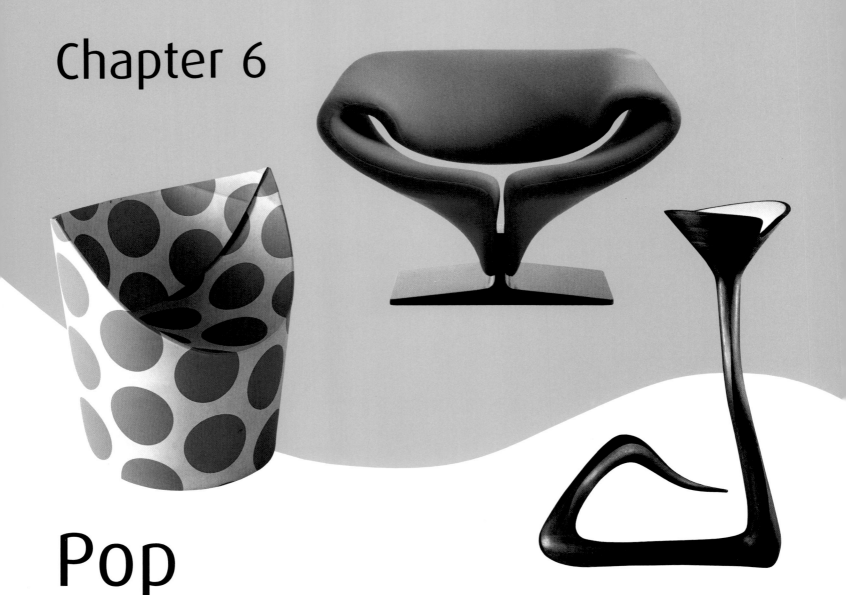

Pop

The Pop culture of the 1960s presented much that was the antithesis of Modernism. Today, we know and accept that technology moves extremely fast, in the 1960s people were just coming to terms with it. This was the decade that saw the birth of youth culture; life was 'hip' and 'cool' and being in fashion was of the utmost importance.

The alternative – being unfashionable – meant that consumers disregarded objects more quickly in search of the next 'in' thing. The public no longer wanted good design which, by its very nature has a longer life span, they wanted fashionable design. As a result, popular culture was swiftly absorbed into the design

vocabulary (note Joe Colombo's baseball glove), and displays of contemporary wit and humour were perfectly acceptable.

Not everything was made to be disposable, but there were many designers who revelled in the departure from the purism of the Modernists. They explored the opportunities that technology and new materials allowed, aided and abetted by the increasingly liberated lifestyle of the 1960s.

The nuclear and mobile society brought smaller homes and apartments which called for multi-purpose furniture: Roberto Matta's 'Malitte' seating system shows a space-saving interpretation of domestic furniture that is also visually

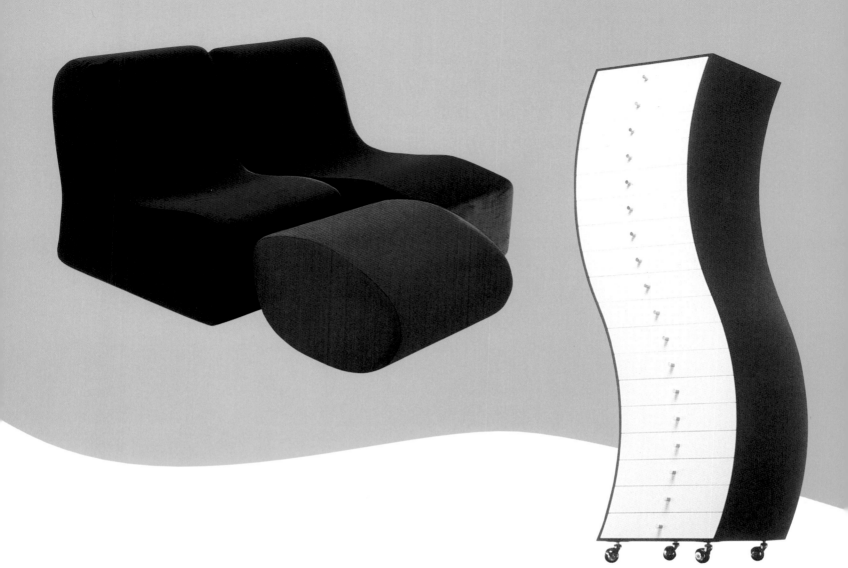

stimulating. The blow-up chair, made from PVC, was another example of new materials permitting new forms, and the demise of the patent on polyethylene was a boon for many designers.

The social and political radicalism of the 1960s evolved into the conscience-stricken 1970s, with its increased concern for the environment. The Environmental Protection Agency was founded in 1970, and many people began to reassess the trend for obsolescence. The American, Victor Popanek, was particularly forceful in his condemnation of consumer goods as the tools of capitalism, and called on architects and designers to take responsibility for shaping a better environment.

With this new-found accountability there was room for diversity. Handcrafted pieces, with their respect for natural materials gained more credence, and conservation was a necessary path following the oil crisis of 1973 and the ensuing global recession in 1975. Designers took to using technology as a server and the slogan became 'Design for Need'.

The new technology and facilities available to designers actually extended the design process, often requiring specialist input from engineers, consumer researchers and ergonomics advisors.

Finally, mass consumerism brought with it consumer rights. The issue of safety became yet another factor in the list of considerations for the designer to account for, other than the aesthetic quality of his work.

Sanluca Armchair And Footstool

Date: **1959**

Designers: **Pier Giacomo Castiglioni (1913–68)**
and Achille Castiglioni (b. 1918)

Made by: **Gavina from 1961**

Normally, a chair – even when it has been designed ergonomically – has a plain, filled-in back to hide the structural elements. Clearly, this is not the case here. The inner walls are padded and shaped, but there is only a thin skin of fabric on the outer ones. The curved sections of the back, sides, seat and rosewood legs have been put together without any attempt to disguise their different purposes.

The Castiglioni brothers, Livio, Pier Giacomo and Achille, all graduated in architecture from the Milan Politecno. Pier Giacomo and Achille collaborated successfully for over 20 years, until Pier Giacomo's untimely death in 1968.

Technically, the brothers' work was very modern. They adhered to functionalist principles and are well remembered for pieces that were inspired by Marcel Duchamps – a leading exponent of Dadaism – which incorporated existing objects into new designs. Thus, we have the T010 lamp (1962), which features a car headlight in a standard lamp, and the Mezzadro stool, which used a tractor seat (1957). Achille and Pier Giacomo both taught at the Milan Politecno, and were significant contributors to post-war Italian design.

Carved Music Stand

Date: *c* 1951–60

Designer: **Wharton Esherick (1887–1980)**

Along with Wendell Castle, American designer, Wharton Esherick helped to keep craft tradition alive in post-war America.

Although he was a skilful cabinet-maker, the style of Esherick's work is modern. Throughout his long career his designs reflected the age in which they were made, and prove that traditional materials and methods do not necessarily produce old-fashioned results.

This walnut and cherry music stand has a sculptural quality, and the spaces created by the configuration of the solid elements are an important factor in its success.

The sheet music is supported by a lattice structure, with slightly curved horizontal bars. The two vertical struts are angled and lined up with the front supports. Stability is added by a third leg at the back and the triangular-shaped under-tier that unites them. The form is based around the easel, and the truncated 'A' is repeated within the sheet music frame. The rounded edges, curved lines and tapered legs give the piece a fluidity and refinement that seems entirely appropriate for a music stand.

'Spotty' Child's Chair

Date: **1963**

Designer: **Peter Murdoch (b. 1940)**

Made by: **International Paper Corporation, New York**

The 'Spotty' child's chair was the first commercially produced paper seat. It is the ultimate expression of the disposable culture – although, paradoxically, the Kraft paper used was recyclable. British designer Peter Murdoch designed the 'Spotty' chair while studying at the Royal College of Art in 1963. He worked in New York the following year, where the chair was put into a limited production run.

The 'Spotty' chair came flat-packed, and was sold in supermarkets and department stores with instructions for assembly. These consisted of folding along specific lines and tucking flaps into slots. The decoration was screen-printed, easy to produce and colourful to look at. The polyethylene, easy-to-clean coating made it more durable in the sticky hands of children, and the chair was also light enough for them to move around.

Plywood Chair

Date: **1963**

Designer: **Grete Jalk (b. 1920)**

Made by: **Poul Jeppersen, Denmark**

By the time Danish designer Grete Jalk produced this imaginative chair, the popularity of plywood was in decline. As a result, the manufacturer only put around 300 into production.

The chair is made from two sheets of plywood, cut and folded to give a distinctive winged form. The feel is Oriental rather than Danish, reminding us of origami, the Japanese art of paper folding.

The resilience of the plywood has allowed the form to remain uncluttered. The simple line would have been spoilt if the back supports had been added as extra pieces, and it is a credit to the aesthetics and technical accomplishment of the manufacturer that it works so well. The chair was also available in a number of different surface veneers including oak, rosewood, walnut, beech, teak and Oregon pine.

Carlton Room Divider

Date: **1964**

Designer: **Ettore Sottsass Jnr (b. 1917)**

Made by: **Renzo Brugalo, Milan**

A highly individual designer, Italian Ettore Sottsass Jnr originally trained as an architect in the rational and functional tradition of the Modernists. However, by the 1950s he had rejected this and his work became the antithesis of functionalism, combining a love of pre-war abstract art with the ideology of Pop art. 'I don't understand why enduring design is better than disappearing design,' said Sottsass. 'I must admit that for me obsolescence is just the sugar of life.'

This 'Mobile de Torre' (Tower Furniture) does not comply with conventional rectangular form. The geometric structure stands at 2.52 m (over 8 ft) tall, and is a mixture of solid and open rectangular shapes.

The Tower Furniture started with a combined desk/cabinet/bookcase, designed by Sottsass in 1960 for the Tchou apartment in Milan. The piece illustrated was not produced until 1981 – 18 years after its conception.

Ribbon Chair

Date: **1965**

Designer: **Pierre Paulin (b. 1927)**

Made by: **Artifort, Netherlands**

Aptly named, the Ribbon chair curves, dips and folds to unite at a central support and stand. Predating moulded plastic forms, the French designer used tubular-steel frames covered with rubber sheeting and foam-rubber padding. In turn, these were covered with a stretch fabric that clung closely to the contours of the foam. The sinuous horizontal form is the epitome of the laid-back 1960s; its breadth and curves allow plenty of room for the sitter to adopt a variety of different positions.

Pierre Paulin is one of France's leading post-war designers. The Ribbon chair won an International Design Award in 1969, and Paulin has executed a number of important commissions, including furniture and interiors for apartments in the Élysée Palace and seating in the Louvre. The designer has also designed car interiors for Citröen and packaging for Christian Dior.

Serpentine Floor Lamp

Date: **1965**

Designer: **Wendell Castle (b. 1932)**

The word Serpentine describes this mahogany
standard lamp perfectly. Standing at 2.24 m
(over 7 ft) tall with its body trailing behind it, the
uplighter shade gapes open like the dislocated
jaw of a snake about to swallow its prey. In fact,
the inspiration for this piece came from the act of
unfolding a paper clip, but its power and strength
is undoubtedly snake-like.

Wendell Castle is an American designer who
continued the craft tradition in a contemporary way.
Rather than use new materials to suggest new forms,
he concentrates on being more imaginative with
conventional ones. As a result, much of his work is
sculptural, with less emphasis on the functional.

However, he has not rejected modern materials
altogether, having produced two furniture ranges in
moulded reinforced polyester; called the Castle and
Molar Groups, they are also very sculptural.

Djinn Chair and Stool

Date: **1965**

Designer: **Olivier Mourgue (b. 1939)**

Made by: **Airborne, France**

This chair and stool employ the same materials that Pierre Paulin used for his Ribbon chair. The nylon stretch jersey that covers the pieces was developed in East Germany in the 1950s and is essential to the success of the design. The material clings tightly to the tubular metal, rubber and foam form, and there is no need for traditional upholstery, which would make the pieces much more expensive to produce.

In designing the Djinn furniture, Frenchman Olivier Mourgue was exploring the possibilities of nylon stretch jersey, as well as producing furniture that was physically and visually light. The range was thought to be sufficiently futuristic by Stanley Kubrick, who used it in his film *2001: A Space Odyssey*. The Djinn range also won an International Design Award in 1965.

'Malitte' Seating System

Date: **1966**

Designer: **Roberto Sebastian Matta (b. 1911)**

Made by: **Knoll**

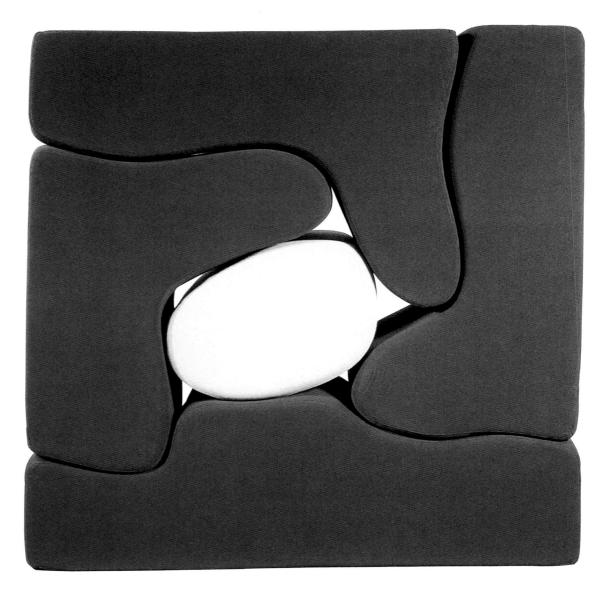

This space-saving seating system is innovative and imaginative. It was designed by Roberto Sebastian Matta who trained as an architect in Chile before moving to Paris. There he worked in Le Corbusier's office for a year before returning to his first love which was painting.

It was as an artist that Matta was invited by Dino Gavina to design furniture. The jigsaw-type seating system was named after his wife Malitte, and looks like a modern work of art when stored. Collectively, the pieces form a visual statement. Separately, they are a versatile group of seats, offering a variety of sitting positions that can be informally arranged. Easily mass-produced in fabric-covered blocks of polyurethane foam, the concept is as impressive today as it was in the 1960s.

Wire Armchair

Date: **1966**

Designer: **Warren Platner (b. 1919)**

Made by: **Knoll**

When Warren Platner set out to design this chair (second left) – part of a group of furniture – his aim was to produce a range that was functional and modern, as well as elegant and graceful.

In addition, the American designer wanted to produce furniture that was decorative without using applied ornamentation; he achieved this through the optical effects created by the multiple rod structures. The broad sweep of the back and sides are open and welcoming, and the upholstery offers comfort to the metal frame. The base shows the metal structure of fine metal rods contained by hoops, and the optical result is the moiré effect, similar to watered silk.

Platner studied as an architect and set up his own architectural and design office in 1965 after working for Raymond Loewy and Eero Saarinen Associates – two of America's most influential twentieth-century designers.

Globe Chair

Date: **1963**

Designer: **Eero Aarnio (b. 1932)**

Made by: **Asko, Finland**

Taking his cue from the high-sided chairs of the late nineteenth century (designed to shield the sitter from draughts as well as provide privacy), Eero Aarnio's Globe chair offers a wonderfully personal cocoon from the outside world.

Born in Helsinki, Aarnio trained as an interior and industrial designer, establishing his own firm in 1962. He embraced new technology and materials, enjoying the scope they offered. The fibreglass-reinforced polyester enabled Aarnio to produce his ball enclosure, but the base and support had to be made in traditional metal to provide additional strength and counterbalance. He later produced a hanging, see-through variation of the Globe chair, called the Bubble chair.

'Floris' Child's Chair

Date: **1967**

Designer: **Günter Beltzig (b. 1941)**

Made by: **Gebruder Beltzig, Germany**

The all-weather 'Floris' stacking chair is part of a range of children's furniture in moulded fibreglass-reinforced polyester, designed by German Günter Beltzig. Unfortunately, because the chair is formed in two pieces, involvement by hand was necessary, making it unsuitable for mass production.

A wonderfully surrealist piece that looks as though it has walked straight out of a Salvador Dalí painting, the chair's unusual shape makes it instantly appealing to the inquisitive minds of children. The organic form fits the contours of the body, the winged shapes on the back give extra support for the neck and lower back of its growing occupants, and the angles of the three legs offer a stable base that cannot be easily tipped over or rocked.

Storage Unit Trolley

Date: **1967**

Designer: **Joe Colombo (1930–71)**

Made by: **Zanotta**

This multi-purpose trolley was commissioned originally so that the company Abet Lamiati could show off their newly-developed laminate. The trolley of square section with rounded corners has 14 levels of laminate cut to various shapes, and these are fixed to four tubular columns. The piece is made mobile by the castors.

The trolley reflects the open approach to storage that was fashionable at the time. Rather than boxing everything in behind closed doors, storage units and bookcases were often left open, displaying a multiplicity of compartments and shelves. The top shelves are appropriate for books, cups and glasses, while the lower more narrowly spaced ones are ideal for paperwork and magazines.

Tablecloth Table

Date: **1969**

Designed by: **Studio Tetrach**

Made by: **Alberto Bazzani**

This table, designed by the Studio Tetrach in Milan, shows the sculptural qualities of plastic – in this case, fibreglass-reinforced polyester. Looking at the photograph, one could swear there was a table underneath, and that the folded drapes were made of soft cloth rather than hard plastic.

The table was designed as a slightly tongue-in-cheek dig at designers and manufacturers who, according to Studio Tetrach, had failed to appreciate the true qualities of plastic, using it only as a substitute for wood. In a letter to the Montreal Museum of Decorative Arts in January 1995, Enrico De Munari explained the

Studio's 'light-hearted reproach to our fellow designers – because by imitating the "ways" of wood and iron, one could end up not only confusing one material with another, taking away their own semantic identity, but even mixing up form and content; that is to say, in our case, tablecloth and table.'

Boomerang Desk and Swivel Chair

Date: **1969**

Designer: **Maurice Calka (dates unknown)**

Made by: **Lelue Deshay**

This Boomerang desk shows the 1960s' treatment of the pedestal desk. Designed by Frenchman Maurice Calka, the rectilinear form is replaced by a biomorphic kidney-shaped top and swollen pedestals which look like they are bulging with their hidden contents.

The traditional leather inset is replaced by a waterproof plastic surface, and the deep drawers on both sides all fit flush to the form – their handles are circular recesses. Thanks to the desk's gently curving form, there are no sharp edges to knock your knees on when the sitter swivels from side to side in the matching chair.

The chair with its plump leather upholstery, similar to that of a bucket seat in a sports car, is supported by an oval-moulded shell back, and raised on a central column with five supports. In 1969 the Boomerang desk was awarded the Grand Prix de Rome.

Chair and Footstool

Date: **1969**

Designer: **Jørn Utzon (b. 1918)**

Made by: **Fritz Hansen, Denmark**

You will have come across the work of this Danish architect and designer before, only his building is so famous everyone has forgotten the creative force behind it.

Jørn Utzon designed the Sydney Opera House, and his approach to furniture design is similarly sculptural. To this end, he was always interested in new technology and materials. He was also known for his additive approach, letting a design evolve as it went along.

The chair and stool are organic and fluid. They were designed as part of a seating system that you could add repeats to, to make a sofa or a longer seating line. There are no sharp edges, just clean lines and a sort of visual rhythm.

The main feature of the plywood chair is the moulded laminate seat and back, which curves down to form the front support, shaped like a question mark. This is upholstered with fabric-covered foam that adds substance to its undulating profile. The tubular-steel support is unobtrusive and angled for comfort and support.

'Wiggle' Side Chair

Date: **1970**

Designer: **Frank O Gehry (b. 1929)**

Made by: **Jack Brogan**

These 'Wiggle' side chairs are part of a series of 17 pieces of furniture called 'Easy Edges'. Apparently, American architect and designer Frank O Gehry became interested in paper furniture when he was creating display pieces for department stores (a suggestion from someone at Bloomingdales led him to pursue the matter).

He researched cardboard and corrugated cardboard thoroughly, and created thick laminated layers that could be folded like ribbons, bent gently or used at right angles. In this thick form it proved remarkably resilient and the texture was like corduroy.

Gehry ended the production of Easy Edges pieces after only three months because the furniture was so popular it was distracting him from his main love, architecture. From the ecologist's point of view it showed what could be done with wastepaper in the hands of an impressive designer.

Chest of Drawers

Date: **1970**

Designer: **Shiro Kuramata (1934–91)**

Made by: **Cappellini**

In an interview conducted for the Italian design magazine *Domus* in April 1984, Japanese designer Shiro Kuramata confessed to a fascination for drawers that extended back to his childhood. 'Mine used to be full of toys and spinning tops and coloured cards; they were my hidden treasures. I loved putting my hand into these untidy drawers and rummaging about,' he said. He subsequently designed them stacked in pyramid shapes, as tables, and even included them in his chair designs.

This chest of drawers shows an interesting deformation of the conventional rectangular chest. Crafted from lacquered and ebonized ash, the serpentine form is slightly unsettling, and makes us reassess a familiar piece of furniture we usually take for granted. The curves add a dynamic element – in contrast to the often more sedentary form.

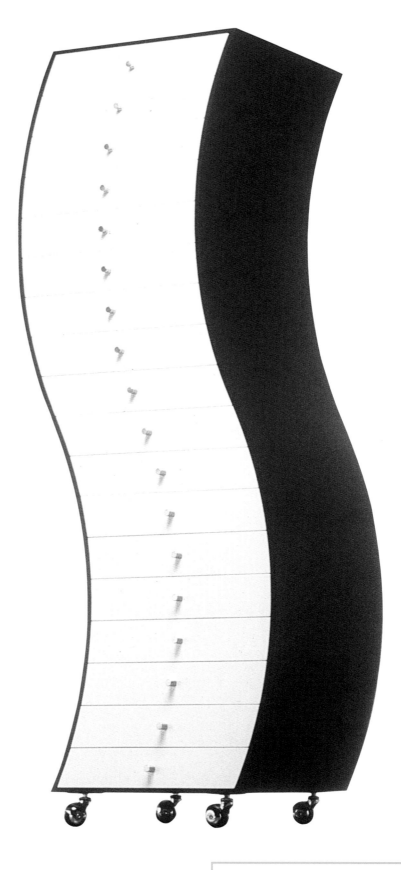

Axe Coffee Table

Date: *c* 1970

Designer: **Unknown**

Oscar Woollens was a progressive furniture shop in North London during the 1960s and 1970s. This unusual aluminium and smoky-glass coffee table was retailed by them but, to date, there is no information about who it was designed by, or indeed who made it.

The table makes a strong visual statement with its unusual-shaped base and contrasting colours and materials. It is essentially very simple, made from a single pane of glass and a single sheet of aluminium. The latter was cut into a circle and three ovals cut out to leave the distinctive shape intact.

The three blade-like shapes have been slightly twisted to form the supports, and three rubber pads enable the glass to sit safely on the metal base. As is so often the case, some of the best designs are also the simplest ones, and this table is a perfect example.

Libro Chair

Date: **1970**

Designed by: **Gruppo DAM (Designers Associati Milan)**

Made by: **Gruppo Industriale, Italy**

The promotion of the Libro chair as the perfect piece of furniture for reading is an excellent example of the wit and freedom of design during the Pop art period. Clearly, the assembly of the Libro has been cleverly thought out. The form is modelled on an open book, with ten pages, and a fixed cushion in the centre. Each of the individual pages or cushions can be turned, thus altering the seating position for the occupant from upright to reclined, as well as varying stages in-between.

The chair's aluminium frame and canvas covering can be adjusted in height by increasing or decreasing the acuteness of the angle. The vinyl upholstery was the height of fashion at the time, while the contrasting colours add emphasis to the form.

'Joe' Sofa

Date: **1970**

Designers: **Gionatan De Pas (b. 1932), Paolo Lomazzi (b. 1936) and Donato D'Urbino (b. 1935)**

Made by: **Poltrovna, Italy**

The 'Joe' sofa is a good example of popular culture entering the design vocabulary of the early 1970s. It is a very comfortable seat that was also fun and fashionable. In America Joe DiMaggio was known as a great baseball player, but to the rest of the world he was more famous for marrying Marilyn Monroe.

Whether there is any witty reference to the sitter being in 'safe hands' is unrecorded, but the glove form, created by three Italian designers, was reputedly inspired by the large and surreal sculptures of Claes Oldenburg. It is approximately 1.05 m (3 ft 5 in) high, 1.68 m (5½ ft) wide, and 86 cm (2 ft 10 in) deep, and the stitched leather cover is filled with polyurethane foam. The leather is also stamped with the designer's facsimile signatures, in the same way that sports endorsements are embossed on real baseball gloves.

'Marilyn' Chair

Date: **1972**

Designer: **Arata Isozaki (b. 1931)**

Made by: **Tendo, Japan**

This chair is another example of 1970s culture impacting on design. Presumably the piece takes its name from Marilyn Monroe, with its curvaceous outline and tapered legs suggesting a shapely ankle.

On a more serious note, the high-backed beechwood form owes much to the earlier works of Charles Rennie Mackintosh and Frank Lloyd Wright, who both produced classic high-backed chairs. The upper part of this chair is curved in exactly the right place to support the lower back, but the leather-covered seat, front legs and stretchers are very angular in order to emphasize the fluidity of the back.

Japanese architect and designer Arata Isozaki's sense of humour is well known. As the architect of the Team Disney Building in Florida, he managed to incorporate cartoon motifs into the structure, including a porch with the stylized outline of Mickey Mouse's ears.

Banana Sofa

Date: **1972**

Designer: **Unknown**

In 1972 the Dole Banana Company held a competition for a piece of furniture to be designed with bananas as the theme. This amusingly gimmicky sofa was awarded first prize, and reflects the lack of restraint on design at the time – in keeping with similarly irreverent pieces like the Libro chair and the 'Joe' sofa.

Made in substantial polyurethane foam, the sofa's seat and back are formed in the shape of a bunch of three bananas and covered in yellow stretch fabric. The ends are coloured brown and the Dole label is incorporated on the side in much the same way as a sticky label on a real piece of fruit. The fact that the sofa was made for an overtly commercial end does not diminish its effect, although it does give an indication of the increased pressures of commercialism, and in particular the designer label which came to the fore at the end of the twentieth century.

Sitting Wheel

Date: **1974**

Designer: **Verner Panton (1926–98)**

Verner Panton seriously challenges our preconceptions of the chair with this highly innovative form. The Sitting Wheel was never put into full production, presumably because of its commercial limitations, but its appeal is without question. In the photograph, the Danish designer illustrates the chair's casual feel and freewheeling versatility that makes it seem particularly suited to large open spaces.

The Sitting Wheel is made from a dense foam so that the weight of its occupant does not distort the shape or interfere with its rocking and rolling ability. The foam is covered with a close-fitting fabric which, had the wheel been put into production, would have been available in a variety of cheerful colours.

Chapter 7

Postmodernism

Although design had been moving away from the purist theories of Modernism for some time, it wasn't until the late 1970s and early 1980s that Postmodernism was born. The Studio Alchimia under the leadership of Alessandro Mendini, and the Memphis Group inspired by Ettore Sottsass Jnr, actively rejected ascetic Modernism. Postmodernism was radical, inventive and over the top.

The home of Postmodernism was Italy where there were enough quality manufacturers who could produce limited-edition designs. The Alchimia and Memphis groups both embraced ornamentation, but where the Alchimia favoured the influence of past design, Memphis concentrated on the present and the future.

The Studio Alchimia showed their often humorous opposition to rational design by taking everyday objects and applying various forms of decoration, for example a Wassily chair by Marcel Breuer was painted with cloud-like additions. They showed a group of items under the title of 'Bau. Haus', although it could not have been further removed from the functionalist principles expressed by the original design school (see Chapter 3). Studio Alchimia was an experimental group producing expensive, craft-orientated pieces. They were in favour of sentiment, nostalgia and emotion.

Memphis was openly more commercial. When they had their first show in 1981 they sold themselves as 'Memphis, The New

International Style', and since the group included leading designers from America, Japan, Italy, Spain, Austria and Britain, the international claim was a valid one. There was no pre-set theme to the work of either groups – it simply had to be modern, progressive and decorative, although it was branded by some critics as lacking in moral integrity. Alchimia was chided for its shallow use of past styles, and Memphis for exploiting popular culture, viewed by some critics as an unimpressive source.

Italian design and manufacturing was not the only show worth watching, however. The craft tradition was quietly kept alive in England by the Barnsley Workshops and the increasingly acclaimed designs of John Makepeace. In America, Wendell Castle was producing modern design using craft skills. Leading designers were also exploring old materials with new ideas, such as Frank O Gehry and his range of woven-wood furniture.

Overall, the sculptural qualities of furniture were being increasingly explored – partly because the flexibility and range of materials allowed it, and partly because designers were looking for new ways to express themselves outside conventional forms. In the pre-recession 1980s there was enough money to sponsor new and exciting furniture design. It was the heyday of the image-conscious yuppie, and unusual sculptural pieces or way-out Italian design was totally in keeping with its image. By the mid-1980s, Postmodernism was already running out of steam, evolving from its reactionary stance against Modernism into a style that was less strident and more diverse.

Proust's Armchair

Date: **1978**

Designer: **Alessandro Mendini (b. 1931)**

Made for: **Studio Alchimia**

When asked about the title of these chairs, Italian architect and designer Alessandro Mendini explained that he wanted to create something Marcel Proust would have been happy to sit in. The heavily-carved frame with its elaborate scrolls and openwork was hand-painted in a pattern inspired by the brushwork of the Impressionists (apparently, Proust was a collector).

In 1976 Mendini had designed fabrics for Cassina on the theme of Marcel Proust, and he incorporated his work into comfortable upholstery for this chair.

The chair is from a collection of what Mendini termed as 'Redesigns', in which he reinterpreted items from the past without totally extinguishing their historical identity. The chair's carved baroque form with its pointillist surface would not have been cheap to buy, and the patterns and colours on each version of the chair are different. Mendini's aim was to promote craftsmanship, decoration and symbolism, following what he viewed as the drought years of clinical Modernism.

Bronze and Glass Dining Table

Date: *c* 1980

Designer: **Diego Giacometti (1902–85)**

In keeping with the sculptural qualities of Post-modernist pieces, Swiss decorative artist and sculptor Diego Giacometti offers a perfect combination between furniture making and sculpting. In 1933 he, and his more famous brother Alberto, were asked by the French decorator Jean-Michel Frank to design and make lamps and furnishings for his clients. At this stage it was thought that Alberto played a more creative role, while Diego took responsibility for structure and casting.

Alberto Giacometti was essentially a fine artist; he left his brother to carry on in the field of decorative and applied arts, where Diego's love of nature is particularly obvious. The table stands at 75 cm (2½ ft) high and the thick glass top has a diameter of 1.52 m (5 ft).

At the top of the bronze base, with its textured surface and verdigris patina, there are four frog finials which secure the glass. The frame just beneath the glass has a band of gilt highlighted lily-pad leaves, and the cross-stretchers beneath this are cast with two small birds and a dish. The piece is also stamped 'Diego'.

Sunset in New York Sofa

Date: **1980**

Designer: **Gaetano Pesce (b. 1939)**

Made by: **Cassina, Milan**

This sofa is such a clever idea and works brilliantly with the colours and choice of fabric. It has a plywood frame and base, the former of which is covered with polyurethane foam and orange fabric. The cushions are cleverly covered in two-tone embossed fabric that gives the impression of windows and walls. From soft furnishings Gaetano Pesce has managed to create a romantic visual statement based on New York's famous skyline. The only downside is that when people sit down, they immediately reduce the visual impact.

Pesce is an innovative modern designer who constantly strives to make the most of new technology and materials – especially in terms of design and production method. For example, he has created chairs from felt, coating the material in varying amounts of resin to alter the levels of rigidity. Pesce also believes there is a demand for limited editions and one-off pieces, and that there is no reason why the technology of new materials and mass production should impede us from doing this at more economically viable prices.

Plaza Dressing Table and Stool

Date: **1981**

Designer: **Michael Graves (b. 1934)**

Made for: **Memphis**

American architect and designer Michael Graves converted from 'white-Modernist' architecture to become a leading exponent of Postmodernism. He practised what he termed 'figurative' design which allowed him to incorporate colour, themes and historic motifs. Prior to designing this piece for Memphis, his furniture was commissioned by the clients of his own buildings.

This dramatic dressing table has an Art Deco feel to it, and this is highlighted by the stepped form and blond briar veneer which contrasts with the turquoise lacquer. The piece extends from its everted plinth base through the steps of drawers, table top and mirror frame and up to the triangular peak. The superstructure is set with tiny light bulbs and a pair of globular shaded lights either side of the circular mirror. This dressing table and stool is not a piece of furniture for shrinking violets!

'Nirvana' Armchair

Date: **1981**

Designer: **Shigeru Uchida (b. 1943)**

Made by: **Chairs Tokyo**

The upper part of this chair is clinically Modernist, with its tubular steel, combined back rail and armrest, which is raised on baked melamine-coated steel rods. The legs are united by cross-stretchers, which also support the fabric-covered seat. It is all very minimalist until one reaches the floor, where one can truly claim to be surprised. Follow one of the front legs as it extends in a sinuous, convoluted ribbon, and watch it evolve into one of the back legs.

In a letter to the Montreal Museum of Decorative Arts in 1995, the Japanese designer explained the form and title of his chair: 'In the Orient, meditating while seated means to enter Nirvana, and its seat represents the sacred space.' The unusual base of his chair was inspired by the Renge-Za – the Lotus flower seat of the Buddhists. 'The Lotus flower is the beautiful entity which reflects brightly against the muddy water, that is, the chaos of today's society,' Uchida continues. 'It is a metaphor unique to the Orient, expressing the relationship between society, human beings and nature.'

Marilyn Sofa

Date: **1981**

Designer: **Hans Hollein (b. 1934)**

Made by: **Poltronova, Italy**

Even without the name of this sofa as a guide, one can guess the inspiration behind the design. After all, who isn't familiar with the image of Marilyn Monroe in the film *The Seven Year Itch*, standing above an air vent, her skirt blowing suggestively around her legs.

The sofa is constructed from a maple root wood, which balances with the soft tones of the satin upholstery stretched over polyurethane padding. The generous curves and open aspect convey tremendous femininity. The back and sides are spread like a sunburst, encapsulating Arthur Miller's observation that Marilyn was like, 'a radiating force lighting up a vast surrounding plain of darkness'.

Hans Hollein, an Austrian architect and interior designer, opened his practice in Vienna in 1964. In 1985 he won the Pritzker Architecture Prize, and was cited by the jury as a 'master of his profession', who 'in the design of museums, schools, shops and public housing ... mingles bold shapes and colours with an exquisite refinement of detail, and never fears to bring together the richest of ancient marbles and the latest in plastics'.

Boxing Ring Tawaraya Seating Area

Date: **1981**

Designer: **Masanori Umeda (b. 1941)**

Made for: **Memphis**

This piece of conceptual furniture was designed for the first Memphis show which shocked the design world in 1981. It is challenging thanks to its departure from preconceived notions about how furniture should look.

It has been suggested that Japanese designer Masanori Umeda juxtaposed East and West in this piece, combining the serenity of a Japanese interior, complete with tatami matting, with the latent violence of the boxing ring. The wooden frame is decorated with a striking monochrome border and the corner supports for the 'ropes', surmounted by lamps with glass globes, also alternate in black and white. The starkness of the frame is softened by silk cushions in shaded colours.

The seating area was created as a conversation 'pit' and is ideal for talkers of a pugnacious nature, while those inclined towards witty banter can indulge in a pillow fight. An alternative version of the seat – minus the central serving surface – was designed as a bed.

'Charly' Armchair

One could never call this painted polyester chair nondescript. In fact, the sensation of being watched takes a little getting used to, although 'Charly' does come in handy if you inadvertently end up with 13 for dinner.

French designer Niki de Sainte-Phalle has always been fascinated by the ancient civilizations of India, Egypt and Mexico – in particular their use of human and animal forms in ritualistic and everyday objects. In her own work, monsters and human and animal forms recur repeatedly. For her, Charly (named after a friend), should be treated as a surprise visitor of the benevolent kind.

In 1996 de Sainte-Phalle wrote a letter to the Montreal Museum of Modern Art, recording her thoughts on Charly and another figurative chair called Clarice: 'They confuse the seat and the sitter, merging the identity of the two. I also like the idea that Clarice and Charly bring to mind childhood memories of comfort or awkwardness when sitting in the lap of an adult.'

Date: **1981**

Designer: **Niki de Sainte-Phalle (b. 1930)**

Made by: **Plastiques d'art R Haligon, France;**

limited edition 5/20

Odalisque Chair

Date: **1985**

Designer: **Allen Jones (b. 1937)**

Made for: **Waddington Galleries, London**

Allen Jones is known for his erotic, occasionally fetishist, furniture, which confirms the feminist view of the exploitation of women in art. This chair is more abstracted and interesting than Jones's dumb-looking mannequins of the 1960s and 1970s, however. Then, the British sculptor dressed his models in leather pants, high-heeled boots and long gloves which, predictably, appealed to men more than to women.

The seat of the Odalisque chair is made from pieces of lacquered birch-veneered laminate, cut to represent elements of the human body – including the legs, torso, head, hair and arms – and assembled accordingly. The chair's multi-faceted construction offers a multitude of interesting perspectives and profiles when viewed from different angles. It is sculpture as furniture or furniture as sculpture.

Nomos Work Table

Date: **1986**

Designer: **Sir Norman Foster (b. 1935) and Foster Associates**

Made by: **Tecno, Milan**

Norman Foster's office furniture system was not a particularly new concept when he designed it in 1986 but it was, and still is, distinctly high tech.

Offering low platforms for computer consoles, and higher ones which could be added or removed for books or files, the chromium-plated steel tubing combined with glass echoes the exposed structure of the Hong Kong and Shanghai Bank, which Foster designed in 1985.

In addition, the British architect and designer also developed a 'vertebrae' system for Nomos, which consisted of a series of articulated plastic clips. These attach to the tubular-steel supports, and help to protect and control the numerous cables that have become an unavoidable hazard of office life.

Audio-Visual Cabinet

Date: *c 1986*

Designers: **David Linley (b. 1961)**

and Matthew Rice (dates unknown)

This audio visual cabinet is an example of the classical influence on Postmodernist design – a style termed by Charles Jencks as 'canonic classicism' in his book *Post Modernism, The New Classicism in Art and Architecture*.

Standing at just over 2.5 m (8 ft) tall, not quite 1.5 m (5 ft) wide and 60 cm (2 ft) deep, it was created by David Linley and Matthew Rice. Together, the two British furniture designers constructed the piece in two parts. The base is approximately one third of the whole, thus complying with the classical, 'golden section' theory of proportion.

The carcass is made of MDF, and serves as a stable base for the natural and stained veneers. The main decorative motif for the marquetry is the stylized columns that dominate the two upper doors and the sides. The interior has an arrangement of sliding shelves and storage compartments, designed to meet the demands of the electronic age.

How High the Moon Armchair

Date: **1986**

Designer: **Shiro Kuramata (1934–91)**

Made by: **Vitra**

This nickel-plated rib mesh chair represents the work of a truly original Japanese designer, renowned for his unusual choice of materials.

Shiro Kuramata always loved working with transparent materials, or ones that gave the illusion of transparency. Here, the large number of holes in the mesh allows the viewer to see the space inside the form (a most unusual claim in chair design), in stark contrast to the symmetry and hardness of the metal. The optical effect of the mesh creates an additional moiré pattern, with a similar appearance to watered silk. When it is illuminated, the armchair takes on a noble and mysterious persona, with light piercing through the holes of the body.

Varius Dining Table

Date: **1986**

Designer: **Oscar Tusquets (b. 1941)**

Made by: **Casas, Spain**

Over the past 20 years there has been a resurgence in Spanish design, mostly originating from Barcelona. Oscar Tusquets is one of the country's leading architects and designers, and this unusual-looking table reflects the new modernity.

The thick glass top, with bowed sides and concave ends, is patterned on the underside with angled parallel lines that meet at the centre to suggest a seam. This is accentuated by the cross-frame beneath, which runs down the centre of the

table. The frame is made of green-stained wood, with triangular skirts uniting the four supports and enclosing the space beneath them. The table is raised on four cast-bronze feet – a modern-day version of the ball-and-claw foot.

Planka Chair

Date: *c* 1986

Designers: **Borge Lindau (b. 1932) and**

Bo Lindekrantz (b. 1932)

Made by: **Lammhults, Sweden**

These chairs look as though they have been assembled from junkyard scraps. The laminated plywood backs could be a piece of rejected packing case, the tubular-steel headrest an old paint roller, and the seat and base bits of scrap metal. The design looks like a political statement, or a dig at our wasteful society, but it was neither. Swedish designers Borge Lindau and Bo Lindekrantz described the Planka chair as 'functionalist romanticism' – their aim was to simplify the seat to its ultimate point.

The two designers met at the Gothenburg School of Arts and Crafts, and established their own practice in 1964. Later, they joined forces with Lammhults, the manufacturer of their successful Opal chair, which they designed in 1965. The Planka chair is not typical of the designers' work, which is more usually characterized by simplicity and a timeless quality, but it does highlight their innovation. In 1969 they won the prestigious Lunning Prize for outstanding contribution to Scandinavian design.

Gloria Sofa

Date: **c 1986**

Designer: **Elizabeth Browning Jackson (b. 1948)**

Made by: **Art et Industrie, USA**

Liquid and molten are the best words to describe the Gloria sofa, created by American designer Elizabeth Browning Jackson.

The sinuous outline of the asymmetric form is made of sculpted foam and resin, the lacquered surface of which helps to make the sofa 'glow'.

The dark motifs, which appear to be airborne on the back and seat of the sofa continue the theme of movement, helping to disturb the pallid block of colour. The complementary colour of the tapering metal supports, and their seeming frailty, helps to accentuate the sofa's inflatable look.

Jackson was part of a group of American artists, designers and sculptors called Art et Industrie, who exhibited regularly at a New York gallery. The group brought together young people who were interested in creating innovative design through a combination of disciplines.

Three-Legged Table

Date: *c* 1986

Designer: **Shiro Kuramata (1934–91)**

Made by: **Ishimaru, Tendo and Top Tone, Japan**

Shiro Kuramata was fascinated by transparency and loved using materials that were either see-through, or allowed a degree of transparency. By nature, furniture is solid, and although the glass and metal mesh used for this table are rigid, their transparency implies frailty.

The triangular top with its rounded corners is made of float glass; the green tone is due to the iron content of the sand. The colour and shape are emphasized by the stepped edge that catches and reflects the light. Kuramata is playing with our preconceived ideas of furniture, presenting a fragile glass top on spindly legs that you can see through. In reality, the glass is toughened for safety's sake, and the mesh metal is surprisingly strong.

Transformer Robot Steel Desk

Date: *c* **1987**

Designer: **Fred Baier (b. 1949)**

This extraordinary piece is reminiscent of the Robinson's talkative robot in the film *Lost in Space* in the 1960s. It is cleverly fashioned with steel supports for strength and stability. Most of the upper section is made from painted and stained birch plywood, which gives visual rather than physical weight.

At the top of the desk, there are angled and open shelves above a roll-top compartment. The writing surface is flanked by twin flaps, and below this is a curved and ribbed area which encloses a filing cabinet and some small drawers. The desk's broad tubular legs extend outwards and terminate with girder-like feet.

English designer Fred Baier is known for his bizarre furniture, and often leaves people guessing as to his intent. This prototype desk was constructed in 1987 while Baier was lecturing at American designer, Wendell Castle's school in New York. It was subsequently chosen to represent British design in the USA and Japan.

Mariposa Bench

Date: **1989**

Designer: **Riccardo Dalisi (b. 1931)**

Made by: **Zanotta, Milan; limited edition 2/9**

When Riccardo Dalisi designed this bench in painted steel he wanted to produce a sculpture, as well as a seat. His theory was that benches are commonplace, so why not create something visually stimulating at the same time. In his view, if it failed as a chair, it would, at least, have succeeded as a work of art.

Dalisi based his argument on the trend for accumulating bric-a-brac. If people were interested in collecting things, then new design possibilities followed. He has intentionally produced something which could be bought as a collector's piece.

Producing a limited edition of nine, Dalisi has added to the bench's rarity value for future collectors. The fact that he painted it himself, also adds to its overall desirability.

Boomerang Sofa

Date: **1989**

Designer: **Massimo Iosa Ghini (b. 1959)**

Made for: **Moroso, Italy**

Since his first collection for Moroso in 1989, Massimo Iosa Ghini's work has attracted a lot of interest. The Italian designer was a professional cartoonist from the early 1980s, and perhaps this is why his work has such a confident line. The Boomerang sofa is fluid and bold – one can happily visualize the artist creating its shape on paper, with clean swift strokes of the pen.

Because of the broad sweep of the upholstered seat, extending without break to form the front supports, the sofa projects an active sense of movement. This is nothing like the rectangular ordinary form most of us have in our sitting rooms.

Boomerang Chair

Date: **1989**

Designer: **Susan Golden (dates unknown)**

Designed for: **Fiell, UK**

This chair has the vitality of primitive Aboriginal art, while also being innovative and modern. It is as much a sculpture as a 'useful' object and recalls Alexander Calder's mobile structures.

British designer Susan Golden works in a variety of materials and finishes, and this chair is a typical example. At first sight, its construction appears uncomplicated, but on closer inspection its complex assembly of boomerang shapes reveals a different textural finish on each surface. Overall, it looks like a compilation of 'dancing' strips of enamelled aluminium, welded together and frozen in motion. As the viewer walks around the chair, its appearance changes constantly.

Millennium Armchair

Date: **1988**

Designer: **John Makepeace (b. 1939)**

Made by: **Alan Amey at John Makepeace Ltd**

This glorious chair, with its spider-web back and curved legs, is beautifully made. Like the great eighteenth-century craftsmen, English designer John Makepeace has made full use of the shapes created by the openwork back. The form is so organic that each of the arched horizontal splats look as though it has evolved from the base bar. In addition, each element of the chair has been rounded to imitate the softening effects of time.

According to a letter from Makepeace in 1999, the purpose of the design was 'to use the three-dimensional flexibility of laminated timber to follow the curvature of the body and give support at the crucial points for good posture and comfort. Every component of the chair was made in this way, giving extraordinary strength and lightness. The larger sections are comprised of 40 consecutive layers, and the small sections of nine laminations.'

Aluminium 'Wing' Chair

Date: **1989**

Designer: **Mark Brazier-Jones (b. 1956)**

The sculptural form of this aluminium chair explores design during the French Empire. The lavish properties, effected by New Zealander Mark Brazier-Jones, would have made Napoleon proud.

The distinctive winged back of the chair is supported on two shaped uprights; together they merge to form the back leg which terminates with a small hoop and an arrow. The plump upholstered seat with its distinctive profile has two extraordinary front supports that look like the legs of some fantastical creature, with claw-and-ball feet.

Brazier-Jones has taken his inspiration from an earlier style, but his aluminium chair is no slavish copy of another designer's work. Like much modern furniture, it relies on sculptural form and space to express itself beyond the limits of its function.

Chapter 8

Into the Millennium

Having left some of the bright colour and unrestrained form of the Postmodernists behind, an interesting legacy remains at the time of the new millennium. However, it is difficult to pick out real styles in the present day without the conviction of hindsight.

Most of the pieces illustrated in this chapter – with the exception of a couple – are more minimalist and less aggressive than those featured in Chapter 7. Instead, they represent the functional, the fantastic, the clever and the poetic – coming from an internationally diverse group of artists who represent the pluralism of post-industrial design.

New design is often the result of developing a previous style, or conversely, presenting the complete opposite. It is rarely conceived in isolation, and will be rooted in the society to which it was born. Information technology is transforming our world at an ever-increasing pace. Encyclopaedic reference material is available to anyone with a computer, and now that more people are able and willing to work from home, the office looks set to become a thing of the past.

If there is one feature that united furniture design in the 1990s, it was an enduring sculptural quality. Pieces were

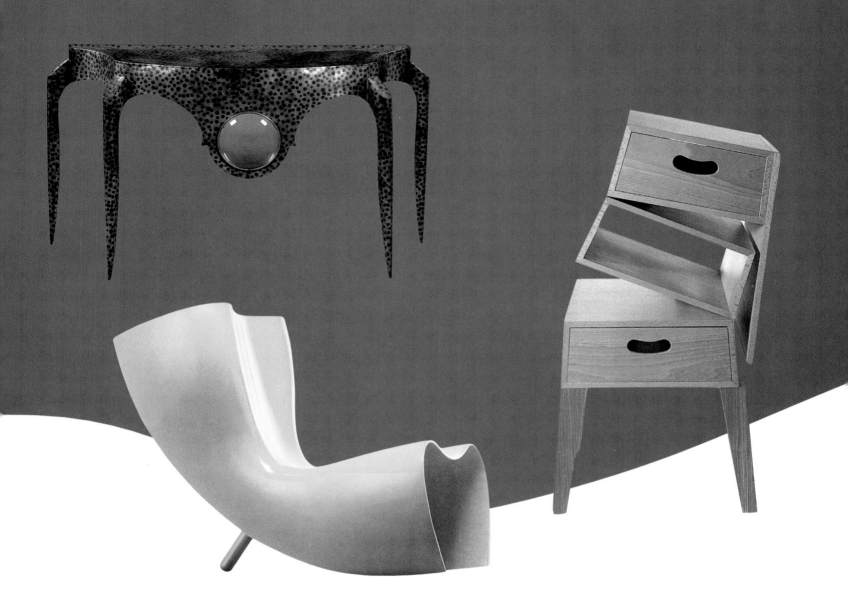

made in a diverse array of materials and expressed a broad spectrum of design influences, but they all had a strong spatial awareness; they could stand alone and be admired and appreciated for something other than their function. For example, Frank O Gehry's comfortable bent and woven-wood armchair has a wonderfully sinuous rhythm to it, creating lots of interesting shapes. Philippe Starck's stool with its simple and organic form contrasts dramatically with the sharper, more dynamic outlines of Philip Wolfson's desk, André Dubreuil's Paris console table and Dakota Jackson's Ke-zu chaise.

Art and design have always been an expression of the society that created it and the diversity of the 1990s can be seen in the decade's furniture. Consumers have become more style-conscious and more appreciative of originality, but there are still a great many pressures on designers before a piece of furniture can finally be brought to the point of production. The 1990s were dominated by a degree of caution brought on by the recession at the beginning of the decade, and compounded by anxious anticipation about what the new millennium might bring.

The furniture in this chapter is poised on the precipice of the twenty-first century. It reflects our feelings of excitement and anxiety as the opportunities of the next century slowly begin to reveal themselves.

Cross Check Armchair

Date: **1989–91**

Designer: **Frank O Gehry**

Made by: **Hasty Plywood and Marshall Group for Knoll, USA**

It took Frank O Gehry several years to develop this chair, together with the technical staff at Knoll International. During the course of its development over 100 full-scale bentwood models were produced in response to the American architect and designer's ideas. The concept for his bentwood furniture had started with an aborted project for the Vitra Design Museum in 1984, and lay dormant until 1989 when Knoll approached Gehry.

The designer's aim was to make bentwood furniture lighter – literally and visually. The open spaces of this chair are as effective as the sinuous fluidity of the wood, which comprises seven layers of maple laminate, each cut to a thickness of 0.8 mm (½₂ in). These are bent and woven to produce a resilient and flexible piece, reminiscent of the sinuous designs of the Art Nouveau period.

Ke-zu Chaise

Date: **1989–90**

Designer: **Dakota Jackson (b. 1949)**

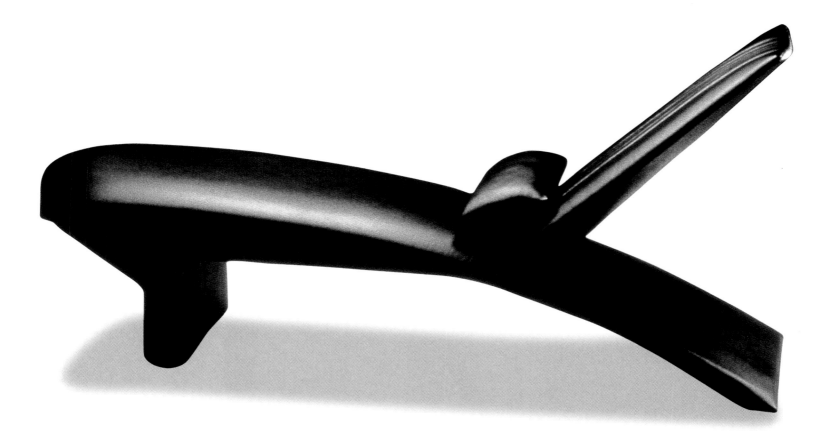

The simple line of the Ke-zu chaise combines an Oriental bearing with an American dynamism, as if the designer developed the streamlined ethic of the 1930s to fulfil a new dimension for the 1990s. The forward projection of the seat, beyond the front support, adds to its dynamism and power. The laminated-wood frame is covered in leather to complete its sophisticated appearance.

Again, we see a distinct sculptural emphasis. Form is obviously important, but not at the expense of the user's comfort. Today's consumers demand good looks and functionability, and Jackson fulfils this design brief by presenting a fluid combination of clarity and elegance with comfort and style.

This chaise was purchased by The Brooklyn Museum of Art in New York as part of their continued commitment to collecting the best of modern applied arts.

WW (Wim Wenders) Stool

Date: **1990**

Designer: **Philippe Starck (b. 1949)**

Made by: **Vitra GmbH, Germany**

There is a calm strength of purpose to this unusual aluminium stool, which the French designer named as is his wont. On first sight it recalls the serene floral photographs of Robert Mapplethorpe but whether the stool resembles a flower or a rhizome, with its roots spreading downwards forming the legs and the broad aerial root forming the backrest, is a matter of opinion.

In the 1980s Philippe Starck became the patron saint of international 'yuppiedom'. He believed that aesthetics are an essential function of furniture, and his enthusiasm for his work made him great at self-promotion. That said, his staggering output has revolutionized the way people think about design.

Starck began his career by designing inflatable furniture and formed the first company to make it. In 1969 he was appointed art director at the Pierre Cardin studio, where he produced 65 furniture designs. In 1982 he was one of the designers selected to refurbish the French president's private apartments in the Élysée Palace. A fine start to a glittering career!

Moonlit Garden Armchair

Date: **1990**

Designer: **Masanori Umeda (b. 1941)**

Made by: **Edra SpA, Italy**

From a European perspective the flower form of this chair recalls the alpine *Gentian*, with its broad petals springing from a small green stem. In fact, it is a *Kikyo* flower (Chinese bellflower) – and one of the Japanese designer's favourites. 'I look forward to seeing it bloom in my little garden every summer,' he says.

There is a sense of folly about this chair, but Masanori Umeda's intentions were anything but frivolous. In his view, 'Modern industrialization in the West, has given priority to function and efficiency, and has destroyed beautiful nature. That's why my design works are full of motifs of animals, plants and nature. It also expresses my hope that people might remember to love creatures and nature in any way through my designs.'

The rich velvet-covered polyurethane foam of this armchair has a natural lushness, contrasting with the small metal ball supports on the tips of the front petals/legs and the mobility castor at the back, all of which link the piece with the modern industrial world.

Bench and Table

Date: **1990**

Designer: **Nanna Ditzel (b. 1923)**

Made by: **Frederica Stolefabrik, Denmark**

Nanna Ditzel has had a long and illustrious career. In 1965 she won the prestigious Lunning Prize together with her husband, who died when he was 43. Her creativity and energy have never diminished, as this visually impressive bench and table illustrate.

The piece takes its inspiration from the graphic beauty of butterflies, both in decoration and form. The two curved backs of the bench are made from maple-veneered plywood, which has been silk-screen printed with concentric bands. The legs and front apron are ebonized and accentuate the linear and curvilinear form, especially when combined with the occasional table. The table is rounded on one edge of its triangular form and slots neatly into the bench, thus completing the visual display.

Chaise

Date: **1990**

Designer: **Tom Dixon (b. 1959)**

Made by: **Dixon PID, UK**

This rush-covered chaise by British designer Tom Dixon resembles a hostage, bound and gagged. His early work, based on components rescued from salvage yards, was assembled with additions of his own making in order to create highly individual pieces.

Dixon graduated in 1978 from the Chelsea School of Art and began designing furniture in 1983.

A self-taught metalworker, his pieces evolve in an organic way. 'My main concerns have to do with elegance of lines and the nature of materials,' he says.

Dixon is representative of today's young designers who take their stimulus from popular culture – music, clubs and theatre – as much as from anticipated areas of influence, such as schools of design.

The eccentric shape of the chaise reflects Dixon's work in the early 1990s. Constantly experimenting with new materials, he has collaborated with architects like Nigel Coates and the Italian manufacturer, Cappellini, with the result that his work continues to evolve with increasing diversity.

'Paris' Steel Console Table

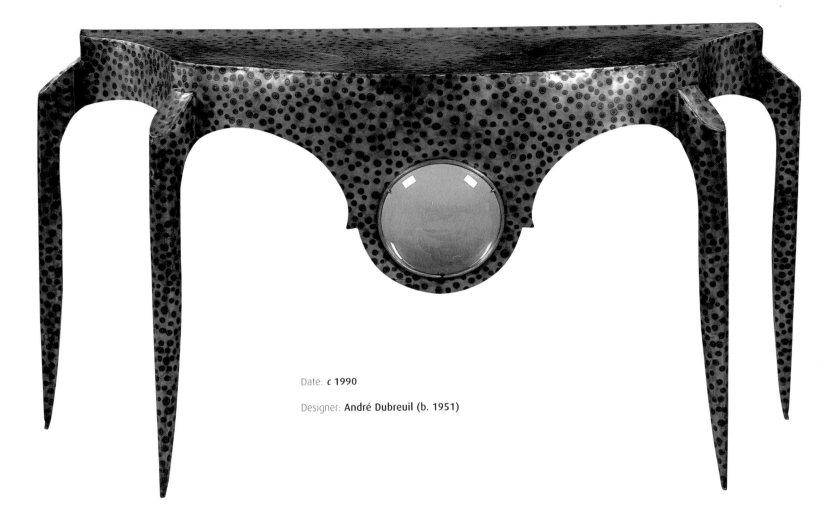

Date: *c* 1990

Designer: **André Dubreuil (b. 1951)**

At first glance this table resembles a predatory insect of mammoth proportions. On closer inspection, however, one sees an extremely elegant console table, recalling the work of Art Deco furniture makers such as Jacques-Emile Ruhlmann.

French designer André Dubreuil's designs fall into the category of New Baroque. He describes his work as the antithesis of 'kitchen furniture' with the latter's paucity of design and lack of inspiration.

His expensive, individual commissions are generally one of a kind, bought as much as a work of art as a piece of furniture. He learned his metalworking skills from fellow designer Tom Dixon, and his pieces are extremely sophisticated.

Numbers of this console table were limited to approximately 40. Each piece was embellished with heat-treated tiny spots resembling the coat of an exotic feline, and supported on legs that taper to fine points, giving a visual lightness. The surface is waxed for a smooth finish and the large glass lens draws the viewer's eye to the heart of the table.

Anthropomorphic Throne Chair

Date: *c* 1990

Designer: **Davy Boyal (dates unknown)**

This extraordinary chair with its demonic wooden horns looks like a medieval instrument of torture. For something so frighteningly predatory it is surprisingly comfortable to sit in, and has been beautifully crafted in wrought iron and wood. It is also higher than it appears in the picture – the sitter has to climb up onto it.

Clearly functioning as a piece of furniture rather than a sculpture, Davy Boyal gives us a perfect example of how far the boundaries between the two can be pushed. Some might argue that he has overstepped the mark, but with an increasing number of designers producing sculptural pieces at the end of the twentieth century, Boyal's throne illustrates how furniture makers can merge their craft with the fine art of sculpture and still produce workable pieces. Perhaps it is from here that we will start the long journey back?

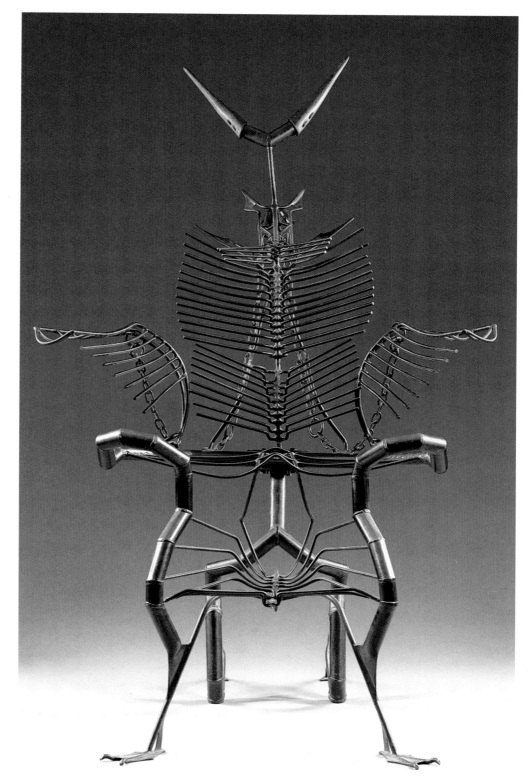

Little Sister Armchair

Date: **c 1990**

Designer: **Roberto Lazzeroni (b. 1950)**

Made by: **Cidue Casa Comunita**

This armchair has the combined appeal of a young sibling and the wanton charm of Lolita. The slenderness of the curved cone-tubing legs and the cast-aluminium arms express vulnerability, while the blue satin-upholstered back rest is, appropriately, the shape of a heart. The seat is the one concession to the Italian designer's earlier use of high-quality woods.

Roberto Lazzeroni has a predilection for curvilinear forms. His designs recall the work of Carlo Mollino and Antonio Gaudí, and often allude to surrealism. His work is consistently elegant, particularly his designs for Cecotti – a company renowned for its superlative craftsmanship. It has been said that his products are art objects, capable of dominating their more prosaic surroundings.

Prototype Desk

Date: **1991**

Designer: **Philip Michael Wolfson (dates unknown)**

The fact that Philip Wolfson is an architect is clearly reflected in the cantilevered sections of this desk, which overlap to make the structure secure.

The avant-garde feel is further emphasized by the American designer's mix of angled and straight elements. The inset leather writing surface (rectangular on a conventional desk) is angled at one end and conceals a compartment underneath. The distinctive linear grain of the Macassar ebony acts as a form of decoration, breaking up large blank areas and complementing the rectilinear form.

The desk also has an interesting rectangular drawer that works on a pivot joint. The drawer is lined with leather and faced in nickel-plated metal. The piece has been compared to the stark and functional designs of the Modernists, who were active during the 1920s and 1930s.

Banana Cabinet

Date: **1991**

Designer: **Wendell Castle (b. 1932)**

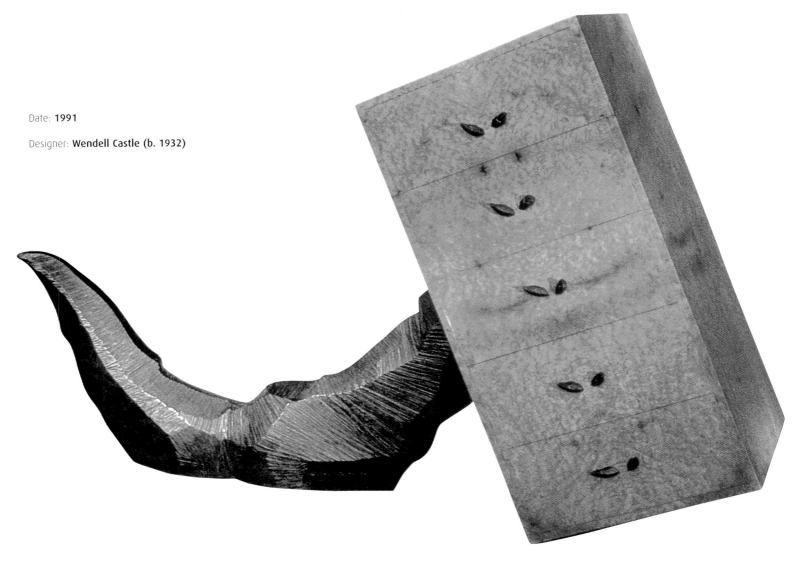

A consummate craftsman in wood, Wendell Castle is the leading exponent of the craft revival in America. In 1980 he founded his own training school, continuing to design furniture in his humorous style (witness his Molar chair, and Chair with Sports Coat). 'I like the idea that things are not exactly what they appear to be, that there's a little bit of deception going on,' he says.

Here, Castle juxtaposes a geometric element with an organic one, forming an uneasy equilibrium. The cabinet is made in a variety of richly-veneered woods and the drawer fronts are punctuated with handles of darker wood. Positioned at a jaunty angle, the cabinet looks as if it is about to topple over, saved only by the roughly sculpted support next to it. But is the dark organic structure reminiscent of a ripe banana, or is the chest indicative of the containers in which the bananas are shipped? Whatever the answer, this is an intriguing example of Castle's imaginative repertoire.

Rocking Chairs

Date: **1992**

Designer: **Sam Maloof (b. 1916)**

Sam Maloof began his artistic life as a graphic designer but converted to furniture in 1949. He made pieces in the craft tradition, and became more widely known in America with the revival of handicraft during the 1970s.

His furniture is characterized by the traditional features associated with the Arts and Crafts Movement – a feeling for materials, quality of construction and 'fitness for purpose' – but with a more organic and contemporary feel.

These rocking chairs are beautifully made in fiddle-back maple and ebony. Their form is conventional, except for the curved back uprights which Maloof extended above the shaped top rail.

One of the main features of the chairs is the back, with its flattened spindles that offer extra support to the sitter's lower back and then taper away. The arms are curved and shaped as if worn by constant use and the seat has sloping ends so the edges don't cut into the sitter's legs. Finally, ebony banding emphasizes the wonderfully fluid line of the rockers.

Three Sofa

Date: **1992**

Designer: **Jasper Morrison (b. 1959)**

Made by: **Cappellini, Italy**

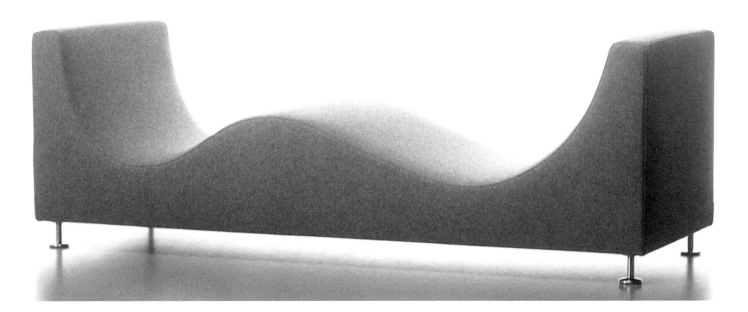

One could never accuse Jasper Morrison of excess, so pared down are his designs. This sofa is totally plain except for its sensual, undulating form. The polyurethane foam emphasizes its sculptural qualities and, thanks to its density, has no need for additional props to help keep its shape. The aluminium frame and supports are discreet, and do not impinge on the sinuous profile. The form poses unusual sitting arrangements – to help the sitter to get up, the sofa has been partly sprung and raised to an appropriate height.

Morrison is an American, who came to England to study at both Kingston School of Art and the Royal College of Art. He also spent a year in Berlin before setting up his own design practice in London in 1986. Morrison's designs are noted for their minimalist qualities, and he tends to produce his pieces in limited runs.

'Patty Difusa' Armchair

William Sawaya was born in Beirut and graduated from the National Academy of Arts there in 1973. In 1978 he moved to Italy and in 1984 he went into partnership with Paolo Moroni. The partnership has produced designs by Michael Graves, Ron Arad and Boris Sipek, as well as pieces by Sawaya.

This extraordinary chair with its sense of fluid control is testament to Sawaya's originality and understanding of the materials – in this case, plywood faced in mahogany. The armrest, which turns into a leg, is not particularly unusual but the fact that it has been executed using a flamboyant ribbon of wood is incredible. This chair needs no ornamentation, its form is everything. In addition, the spaces in and around the chair counter the broad areas of wood and prevent it from appearing too heavy or ponderous.

Date: **1993**

Designer: **William Sawaya (b. 1948)**

Made by: **Sawaya & Moroni**

One Way or Another Bookcase

Date: **1993**

Designer: **Ron Arad (b. 1951)**

Made by: **One off Limited, London and Marzorati Ronchetti Srl, Italy**

Who says a bookcase has to be rectangular? Certainly not Israeli designer Ron Arad, whose concept of storage resulted in this flexible unit. The idea that your bookcase expands in keeping with your mind is an attractive one: for example, a sudden interest in cookery or sailing could totally change the form of the piece, while a clear-out will make it taller and narrower. There are very few furniture designs that change and adapt in such an organic way. This bookcase is quite different to unit furniture, which can only be added to with repeats of the same geometric shape.

Arad's medium is metal which he somehow manages to always make inviting. His work is sculptural, and although he is best known for furniture, he has also undertaken interior projects such as the Tel Aviv Opera House in 1990.

Ring Table

Date: **1993**

Designer: **Danny Lane (b. 1955)**

Aside from architectural commissions it is rare for an artist to work on large-scale projects like this one. As a result, American sculptor Danny Lane leapt at the chance to produce a table which can be sited indoors or out. The irregular form of this piece encourages interaction among its guests, unlike the more typical rectangular banquet table. As a party table it is fun to mingle in and around.

This installation work was assembled for a one-man show at the Economist's Plaza in London in 1993.

Each of the pillars is formed from stacked segments of tempered float-glass around a metal core. The top is made of rectangular pieces of float-glass, that have been tempered, cut and arranged as a kind of collage. An annular ring unites the pillars and top together, and additional metal brackets are used to secure the satellite sections.

It was a major task to assemble these pieces, but apparently the artist enjoyed the challenge immensely, viewing the table as his 'enchanted lego.'

Felt Chair

Date: **1994**

Designer: **Marc Newson (b. 1962)**

Made by: **Cappellini,**

Italy

The concept of people sitting on chairs that bear the ghost of the human form is an interesting idea but not a new one. What makes this piece so striking is Australian designer Marc Newson's choice and treatment of materials, so that it looks as if there is just skin with the filling left out.

Most unusually the fibreglass-reinforced polyester shell curves back and under to form the supports. This highlights the trapped empty space beneath the seat, resulting in a design that is the exact opposite of most chairs, which only trap space for the sitter.

Fold-Out Table

Date: **1995**

Designers: **Tomoko and Shin Azumi (dates unknown)**

Made by: **Frank E Bailey, Swaton, England**

This transformer table is reminiscent of the stacking compartments of a traditional Japanese lunch box. It demonstrates the beauty of dual-function furniture and illustrates the Azumis' successful bid to design a piece that transforms from an upright side table to a low coffee table. This has been achieved through the considered placement of the angled sides and hinges. The lower leg on the right is set wide to conceal the support ledge for the central compartment of the coffee table.

As a result of the angled sides, when the piece is opened out into its coffee table form, the outside drawers push in on the inner compartment, making the structure very secure. All in all, this is a simple, practical and clever piece of furniture.

Magic Chair

Date: **1997**

Designer: **Ross Lovegrove (b. 1958)**

Made by: **Fasem, Italy**

British designer Ross Lovegrove graduated from the Royal College of Art in 1983 and worked for several design consultancies before going into partnership with Julian Brown in 1986. This continued until 1990 when Lovegrove set up his own studio, providing designs for leading manufacturers of modern furniture.

The Magic chair is so minimal it barely appears to exist. Lovegrove is a designer who is constantly on the lookout for better design solutions through new materials and technology. That he manages to do so with such grace is testament to his talent. This chair, with its moulded polyurethane seat and tubular aluminium supports, is incredibly light and simple. There are only two uprights supporting the seat, which illustrates the strength of the materials used; as the title suggests, the piece looks like a magical creation.

Windsor Writing Chest

Date: **1998**

Designer: **John Makepeace OBE**

Made by: **Tom Kealy at John Makepeace Ltd**

The final page of this book illustrates the work of John Makepeace, one of Britain's most celebrated contemporary designers. Even though his work is modern, it also shows the spirit of the Arts and Crafts Movement. William Morris was a great admirer of medieval art, and would have appreciated the allusion to heraldry in the chevron pattern on the surface of this writing chest. There are no pretensions to sculpture, here; in terms of form it clearly owes more to conventional furniture design but the finish is strikingly original.

The chest is made of a single colour wood, although it appears to be two colours because the surface has been cut in broad bands that are slightly angled. These peaks and troughs respond to light, thus creating an illusion of two shades of grey in the chevron pattern. The triangular pull handles, standing proud, reflect the reverse image as the light passes across the face of the chest.

The opening pages of this book show the Arts and Crafts ideal of beauty combined with 'fitness for purpose'. It seems fitting, therefore, that we should end with the work of a contemporary advocate of those principles.

Places of interest to visit

UK
Barnsley Workshops, Petersfield, Hampshire
(annual open day usually in October)
Birmingham Art Gallery & Museum, Birmingham
Brighton Museum & Art Gallery, Brighton, Sussex
Charleston, near Lewes, Sussex
Cheltenham Art Gallery & Museums, Cheltenham,
Gloucestershire
Design Museum, London
Glasgow School of Art, Glasgow
Hunterian Museum, Glasgow
Manchester City Art Gallery, Manchester
Standen (National Trust), East Grinstead, Sussex
Victoria & Albert Museum, London
William Morris Gallery, London

USA and Canada
The Art Institute of Chicago, Chicago
Brooklyn Museum, Brooklyn, New York
Cooper Hewitt, National Museum of Design,
New York
Cranbrook Academy of Art Museum, Bloomfield
Hills, Michigan
Los Angeles County Museum, Los Angeles
Montreal Museum of Decorative Arts, Montreal
Museum of Fine Arts, Boston
Museum of Modern Art, New York
Hancock Shaker Village, Pittsfield, Massachusetts
Philadelphia Museum of Art, Philadelphia
Public Museum of Grand Rapids,
Grand Rapids, Michigan

The Sydney & Frances Lewis Collection, Virginia
Museum of Fine Arts, Richmond, Virginia
The Wolfsonian Foundation, Miami Beach, Florida

Germany
Bauhaus-Archiv, Museum fur Gestaltung, Berlin
Hessisches Landesmuseum, Darmstadt
Munchner Stadtmuseum, Munich
Museum Kunstlerkolanie, Darmstadt
Museum Thonet, Frankenberg
Vitra Design Museum, Weil am Rhein

France
Musée des Art Décoratifs, Paris
Musée de L'École de Nancy, Nancy
Musée d'Orsay, Paris

Spain
Museu de les Arts Decorative, Barcelona

The Netherlands
Stedelijk Museum, Amsterdam

Austria
Osterreichisches Museum, fur Angewandte Kunst,
Vienna

Czech Republic
Arts & Crafts Museum, Prague

Denmark
Det Danske, Kunstindustrimuseum, Copenhagen

Selected Bibliography

Ambasz, Emilio (editor), *The International Design Year-book 1986/87*, London, Thames and Hudson, 1986

Anscombe, Isabel and Gere, Charlotte, *Arts and Crafts in Britain and America*, Van Nostrand Reinhold Company Inc., New York, 1983

Arwas, Victor, *Art Deco*, London, Academy, 1980

Bangert, Albrecht and Armer, Karl Michael, *80s style – Designs of the Decade*, London, Abbeville Press, 1990

Bowman, Leslie Greene, *American Arts and Crafts – Virtue in Design*, Los Angeles, Los Angeles Country Museum of Art in association with Bullfinch Press, 1990

Brandt, Frederick R, *Late 19th and Early 20th Century Decorative Arts – The Sydney and Frances Lewis Collection in the Virginia Museum of Fine Arts*, Virginia Museum of Fine Arts, Richmond, Virginia, 1985

Brunhammer, Yvonne and Tise, Suzanne, *French Decorative Art – The Societé Des Artistes Décorateurs 1900–1942*, Paris, Flammarion, 1900

Camard, Florence, *Ruhlmann – Master of Art Deco*, London, Thames and Hudson, 1984

Capitman, Barbara, Kinnerk, Michael D, Wilhelm, Denis W, *Rediscovering Art Deco USA – A Nationwide Tour of Architectural Delights*, New York, Viking Studio Books, 1994

Carruthers, Annette and Greensted, Mary, *Good Citizens' Furniture – The Arts and Crafts Collections at Cheltenham*, London, Cheltenham Art Gallery and Museums in association with Lund Humphries, 1994

Carruthers, Annette, *Edward Barnsley and his Workshop – Arts & Crafts in the Twentieth Century*, White Cockade Publishing, Oxford, 1992

Catalogue: *Architects – Designers Pugin to Mackintosh*, London, The Fine Art Society Ltd with Haslam & Whiteway Ltd, 1981

Catalogue: *The Art Institute of Chicago Museum Studies, Volume No. 2, The Prairie School – Design Vision for the Midwest*, Chicago, Art Institute of Chicago, 1995

Catalogue: *British Art and Design 1900–1960*, London, Victoria & Albert Museum, 1983

Catalogue: *Joseph M Olbrich – 1867–1908*, Darmstadt, Mathildenhohe Darmstadt, 1983

Catalogue: *The Lunning Prize*, Stockholm, National Museum of Stockholm, 1986,

Catalogue: *Mathildenhohe Museum, Darmstadt 1901–1976* (Volume 4), Darmstadt, Mathildenhohe Museum, 1976

Catalogue: *Richard Riemerschmid van Jugendstil zum Werkbund*, Munich, Stadtmuseum Munich, 1982

Catalogue: *Spring 86*, Fine Art Society, London, 1986

Cervert, Francisco Asensio (editor), *European Masters 3 – Furniture & Lamps*, Barcelona, Atrium, 1991

Cooper, Jeremy, *Victorian and Edwardian Furniture and Interiors from Gothic Revival to Art Nouveau*, London, Thames and Hudson, 1987

Coote, Stephen, *William Morris – His Life & Work*, Stroud, Gloucestershire, Alan Sutton, 1995

Cumming, Elizabeth, *Glasgow 1900 – Art & Design*, Amsterdam, Waanders Publishers, Zwolle, Van Gogh Museum, 1992–3

Dormer, Peter (editor), *The Illustrated Dictionary of 20th-Century Designers*, New York, Mallard Press, 1991

Downey, Claire, *Neo Furniture*, London, Thames and Hudson, 1992

Duncan, Alastair, *American Art Deco*, London, Thames and Hudson, 1986

Duncan, Alastair, *Louis Majorelle – Master of Art Nouveau Design*, London, Thames and Hudson, 1991

Duncan, Alastair, *Art Deco Furniture*, London, Thames and Hudson, 1984

Duncan, Alastair, *Art Nouveau Furniture*, London, Thames and Hudson, 1982

Eidelberg, Martin (editor), *Design 1935–1965 What Modern Was – Selections from the Liliane and David M Stewart Collection, Musée des Arts Décoratif de Montreal*, New York, Harry N Abrams Inc., 1991

Eidelberg, Martin (editor), *Designed for Delight – Alternative aspects of Twentieth-Century Decorative Arts*, Montreal, Flammarion, 1997

Eliens, Titus M, Groot, Marjan and Leidelmeijer, Frans (editors), *Avant-Garde Design: Dutch Decorative Arts 1880–1940*, London, Philip Wilson, 1997

Exhibition catalogue, Hayward Gallery, London: *Thirties – British Art & Design Before the War*, London, Arts Council, 1979–1980

Exhibition Catalogue: Mingei, *Two Centuries of Japanese Folk Art*, The Japanese Folk Crafts Museum, 1995

Fiell, Charlotte and Peter, *Modern Chairs*, Cologne, Taschen, 1993

Fiell, Charlotte and Peter, *1000 Chairs*, Cologne, Taschen, 1997

Fiell, Charlotte and Peter, *Modern Furniture Classics Since 1945*, Washington, AIA Press, 1991

Fowler, Penny and Eaton, Mary Anna, *Frank Lloyd Wright – The Seat of Genius: Chairs 1895–1955*, West Palm Beach, Florida, Eaton Fine Art, Inc., 1997

Frayling, Christopher and Catterall, Claire (editors), *Design of the Times: One Hundred years of the Royal College of Art*, Richard Dennis Publications and the RCA, Shepton Beauchamp, Somerset, 1995

Garner, Philippe, *Eileen Gray – Designer & Architect*, Cologne, Taschen, 1993

Garner, Philippe, *Twentieth-Century Furniture*, Oxford, Phaidon Press, 1980

Gere, Charlotte, Whiteway, Michael, *Nineteenth-Century Design – From Pugin to Mackintosh*, London, Weidenfeld and Nicholson, 1993

Glancey, Jonathan, *20th-Century Architecture*, London, Carlton Books, 1998

Goodden, Suzanna, *A History of Heal's*, London, Heal & Son, 1984

Heller, Carl Benno, *Art Nouveau Furniture*, London, Artline Editions, 1990

Hiesinger, Kathryn B and Marcus, George M, *Landmarks of Twentieth-Century Design – An Illustrated Handbook*, New York, Abbeville Press, 1993

Hiesinger, Kathryn Bloom, *Art Nouveau in Munich – Masters of Jugendstil*, Munich, Prestel, 1988

Horn, Richard, *Memphis – Objects, Furniture & Pattern*, New York, Fireside Book, published by Simon and Schuster Inc., 1986

Jackson, Lesley, *The New Look Design in the Fifties*, London, Thames and Hudson, 1991

Jencks, Charles, Post-modernism – The New Classicism in Art & Architecture, New York, Rizzoli, 1987

Kaplan, Wendy (consultant), *Encyclopaedia of Arts & Crafts – The International Movement 1850–1920*, London, Headline, 1989

Kaplan, Wendy (editor), *Designing Modernity – The Arts of Reform & Persuasion, 1885–1945, Selections from the Wolfsonian*, New York, Thames and Hudson/the Wolfsonian, 1995

Kirkham, Pat, *Charles and Ray Eames – Designers of the Twentieth Century*, Cambridge, Massachusetts, MIT Press, 1998

Kragstuhl, Derk, *The Cantilever Chair*, Stuhlmuseum Burg Beverunden, 1998

Lucie-Smith, Edward, *Lives of the Great 20th- Century Artists*, London, Thames and Hudson, 1986

Makinson, Randall L, *Greene & Greene – Furniture and Related Designs*, Gibbs Smith, Peregrine Smiths Books, Salt Lake City, 1979

Mang, Karl, *History of Modern Furniture*, Stuttgart, Abrams, 1978

Marcilhac, Felix, *Jean Dunand – His Life & Works*, New York, Abrams, 1990

Mendini, Alessandro (editor), *The International Design Yearbook 1996*, London, Abbeville Press, 1996

Ostergard, Derek E (editor), *Bentwood and Metal Furniture, 1850–1946*, New York, The American Federation of Arts, 1987

Pina, Leslie, *Fifties Furniture with Values*, Atglen, Pennsylvania, Schiffer Publishing Ltd, 1996

Russell, Frank, Garner, Philippe, Read, John, *A Century of Chair Design*, London, Academy Editions, 1985

Selected Catalogues: Sotheby's London, New York & Monaco; Christie's, London and New York; Bonhams, London; Phillips, London

Sembach, Klaus-Jurgen, *Henry Van de Velde*, New York, Rizzoli, 1989

Sipek, Borek (editor), *The International Design Yearbook*, London, Abbeville Press, 1993

Spalding, Frances, *Roger Fry – Art and Life*, St Albans, Granda Publishing, 1980

Sparke, Penny, *Italian Design – 1870 to the Present*, London, Thames and Hudson, 1988

Starck, Philippe (editor), *International Design Yearbook 1997*, London, Laurence King, 1997

Tarrago, Salvador, *Gaudi*, Barcelona, FIFA Industrias Graficas, 1974

Taylor, Brian Brace, *Pierre Chareau*, Cologne, Taschen, 1998

The Collector's Encyclopaedia – Victoriana to Art Deco, London, Collins, 1974

Volpe, Tod and Cathers, Beth, *Treasures of the American Arts & Crafts Movement 1890–1920*, London, Thames and Hudson, 1988

Watkinson, Ray, *William Morris as a Designer*, New York, Van Nostrand Reinhold Company, 1967

Weber, Eva, *Art Deco in North America*, London, Bison Books, 1985

Weisberg, Gabriel P, *Art Nouveau Bing – Paris Style 1900*, New York, Harry N Abrams Inc., 1986

Wilson, Richard Guy, Pilgrim Diana H, Tashjian Pickran, *The Machine Age in America 1918–1941*, New York, The Brooklyn Museum, 1986

Woodham, Jonathan M, *Twentieth-Century Ornament*, London, Studio Vista, 1990

Zerbst, Rainer, *Antoni Gaudi*, Cologne, Taschen, 1988

Index

Picture Credits

The publishers would like to thank the following sources for their kind permission to reproduce the pictures in this book:

Alvar Aalto Museum/M Kapanen 98

Ron Arad Associates Ltd/Photograph: Erica Calvi 248

Arflex International 163

© Art & Industrie USA 224

The Art Institute of Chicago/Restricted gift of the Graham Foundation for Advanced Studies in the Fine Arts 30

Art Resource, NY/Cooper-Hewitt Museum, Smithsonian Institution 149

Artifort 189

Asko Furniture Ltd 180, 194

Shin & Tomoko Azumi/Thomas Dobbie 251

The Edward Barnsley Workshop 43

Bonhams 155, 159

Bridgeman Art Library/Cheltenham Art Gallery & Museums, Gloucestershire, UK: Writing cabinet in mahogany and holly, designed by Charles Robert Ashbee, made by the Guild of Handicraft, c 1898–9, 15, Cabinet designed by George Jack (1855–1932) and made by Morris & Company c 1902 (mahogany), Armchair with inlay of holly and ebony, designed and made by Eric Sharpe (1888–1966), 1943 (walnut) 42/The Fine Art Society, London, UK: The Kelmscott Cabinet, designed by Charles Voysey (1857–1941) made by F Coote c 1890 (oak), 16/Private Collection, Bonhams, London: Antony Chair, designed by Jean Prouvé (b. 1901), manufactured by Les Ateliers Jean Prouvé, Maxeville, Paris, 1950 (laminated birch and steel) 160, Lounge Chair and Ottoman, 670 & 671, manufactured by Herman Miller, 1956 (plywood, wood, leather and aluminium) 176, Rush Chaise, 1990 (rush and steel) by Tom Dixon (twentieth century) 239

Brooklyn Museum of Art/designated Purchase Fund 110, Collection of Jim Greer and Dyan Economakos 93

Cappellini spa 201, 246, 250

Cassina SPA/Mario Carrieri 212, Oliviero Venturi 89

© Wendell Castle, Inc. 244

Cheltenham Art Gallery & Museum 37, Photography: Woodley & Quick 13, 38

Chicago Historical Society 134

Christie's Images 25, 28, 33, 34, 39, 40, 49, 54, 55, 57, 60, 62, 65, 68, 69, 73, 74, 84, 90, 92, 95, 99, 106, 107, 109, 113, 120, 123, 125, 128, 132, 137, 138, 145, 150, 164, 174, 178, 187, 191, 211, 213, 226, 243

Photo courtesy of Cranbrook Archives 141

Eaton Fine Art 166

Photo courtesy Edra 237

The Wharton Esherick Museum 185

Etude Tajan 86

Fasem International 252

Fiell International Ltd 170, 179, 229

The Fine Art Society, London 26, 96

Fornasetti 169

Galerie Geitel, Berlin 59

Emile Gallé Musée de L'École de Nancy 72

Galerie Yves Gastou 162

Gebruder Thonet GmbH 70, 87, 102

Massimo Iosa Ghini, photo: Tom Vack 228

Glasgow Museums: Art Gallery & Museum, Kelvingrove 17, 21

Fritz Hansen 177, 199

Haslam and Whiteway Ltd 20

Erik Hesmerg 61, 78, 79, 115

Institut Mathildenhohe Darmstadt 63

© 1988 Dakota Jackson Inc. 235

Allen Jones, RA 218

Courtesy Knoll 156, 168, 173, 192, 234/Courtney Communications 193

Lammhults 223

Landeshauptstadt Munchen Kulturreferat 48

Danny Lane Studio 249

Courtesy Roberto Lazzeroni 242

Los Angeles County Museum of Art/Museum Acquisition Fund 29, Gift of Max Palevsky 19, 32, Gift of Max Palevsky and Jodie Evans 23, 31, 35

John Makepeace Furniture Workshop 230/Photographer Mike Murless 253

Manchester City Art Galleries 167

Document Felix Marcilhac, Paris 122

Wolfgang F Maurer/Galerie Objekte, Munchen 195

Poltronova, Montale 204, 215

Courtesy of Musée des Arts Décoratifs de Montreal, Gift of Vivian & David M Campbell. Photograph by Giles Rivest (Montreal) 188, 197, photograph by Schecter Lee (New York) 190

Musée des Arts Décoratifs, Paris 129, 133

Museum of Decorative Arts, Prague 118

National Trust Photographic Library 12

Nordenfjeldske Kunstindustrimuseum 47

Anthony d'Offay Gallery, London 119

Osterreishisches Museum fur Angewandte Kunst Vienna 76

Werner Panton Design, Basle 207

© Photo Charlotte Perriand 1999, 97

Philadelphia Museum of Art 157

Phillips Fine Art Auctioneers 14, 18, 24, 36, 53, 142, 144, 165, 181, 202, 220

Quittenbaum, Kunstauktionen, Munich 64

Race Furniture Ltd 154

Niki de Saint-Phalle 217

Sawaya & Moroni, Milan, Italy/Photographer: Santa Caleca 247

Sotheby's Picture Library 27, 41, 50, 51, 52, 56, 58, 75, 77, 82, 88, 101, 103, 104, 105, 108, 124, 126, 130, 131, 135, 140, 143, 146, 147, 151, 161, 196, 198, 206, 210, 216, 221, 231, 240, 241, 245

Fredericia Stolefabrik A/S 238

Studio 80/Nacasa & Partners Inc. 214

Walter Dorwin Teague Associates, Inc. 112

Tecno SpA 171/Mauro Masera – Nomos Table for Tecno, General view from the side 219

Tecta SpA 83, 94

Tendo & Co. Ltd 175, 205

John Toomey Gallery/Richard Wright 158

Treadway Gallery Inc. 148

Oscar Tusquets Blanca 222

University of California Santa Barbara, Kem (Karl Emanuel Maria) Weber (1889–1963) Airline Chair Los Angeles CA (1934–5). Photograph by Will Connell Architectural Drawing Collection University Art Museum University of California Santa Barbara 111

Virginia Museum of Fine Arts, Richmond. The Sydney & Frances Lewis Art Nouveau Fund. Photo: Katherine Wetzel © Virginia Museum of Fine Arts 66, Gift of the Sydney & Frances Lewis. Photo: Katherine Wetzel © Virginia Museum of Fine Arts 71, 121, 136, 139

Victoria & Albert Museum 127, 186

Photograph courtesy of Vitra Design Museum 85, 184, 200, 203

Ole Woldbye/Pernille Klemp 100, 172

The Mitchell Wolfson Jr Collection, The Wolfsonian/Florida International University, Miami Beach, Florida/Photo: Bruce White 114

Wurttembergisches LandesMuseum 46

XO 225

Yale University Art Gallery/Gift of Mrs Arthur D Berliss, Sr 91

Zanotta 227

Every effort has been made to acknowledge correctly and contact the source and/copyright holder of each picture, and Carlton Books Limited apologizes for any unintentional errors or omissions which will be corrected in future editions of this book.

Picture Research: Jo Alexander, Carla Preston and Claire Taylor

Acknowledgements

We would like to thank Bruce Hunter for introducing us to Carlton Books and Dan Klein for introducing us to Bruce Hunter. Venetia Penfold and Zia Mattocks have been helpful editors, and we must surely thank the many picture researchers from Carlton Books who have gone to great lengths to find the images we requested.

Particular thanks go to Julia Nethersole for typing the manuscript quicker than most people can think and to Margaret Doyle in New York for helping us choose the American designers represented in these pages.

We would also like to convey our gratitude to the following people for their assistance in a variety of ways: Rhoderick Baker, John Benjamin, Andrew Capitman, Kevin Davies, The Danish Embassy, Barbara Deisroth, Graham Gadd, The Italian Institute, Brian Pasmore, Leonard Riforgiato, Usha Subramaniam, Clive Stewart-Lockhart, Danny Lane and John Makepeace for their valuable time, and our son, Kit, for his forbearance in living with piles of books everywhere and not complaining.